KT-546-328

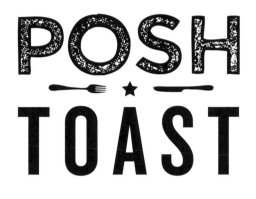

POSH
TOAST

Over 70 recipes for glorious things – on toast

Recipes by Emily Kydd, photography by Louise Hagger,
additional text by Tim Hayward and Sarah Lavelle

QUADRILLE

Publishing Director: Sarah Lavelle
Creative Director: Helen Lewis
Copy Editor: Kate Wanwimolruk
Designer: Gemma Hayden
Photography and Prop Styling: Louise Hagger
Recipe Writer and Food Styling: Emily Kydd
Additional Text: Tim Hayward and Sarah Lavelle
Production: Vincent Smith and Tom Moore

First published in 2015 by Quadrille,
an imprint of Hardie Grant Publishing

Quadrille
52–54 Southwark Street
London SE1 1UN
quadrille.com

Reprinted in 2015 (twice), 2016 (four times), 2017 (three times)
10

Text © Quadrille Publishing Limited 2015
Photography © Quadrille Publishing Limited 2015
Design and layout © Quadrille Publishing Limited 2015

The rights of the author have been asserted. All rights reserved.
No part of the book may be reproduced, stored in a retrieval
system or transmitted in any form or by any means, electronic,
electrostatic, magnetic tape, mechanical, photocopying,
recording or otherwise, without the prior permission in writing
of the publisher.

Cataloguing in Publication Data: a catalogue record for this
book is available from the British Library.

ISBN: 978 1 84949 7008

Printed in China

CONTENTS

— ✦ —

INTRODUCTION

TOAST is a pretty humble food. Perhaps it was the first solid food you were allowed to hold in your hand and post into your own mouth. You probably got melted butter all over your clothes, your face and your high chair – but it's the sheer, unalloyed delight of managing to feed yourself (to the beaming approval of your mum and dad) that imprints toast early in life as most people's favourite food. Everybody loves toast. Don't trust anyone who doesn't.

On the face of it, nothing could be simpler than making toast – a little heat, judiciously applied to scorch a piece of bread. And yet each of us has a set of personal preferences about how toast should be made and served: our own individual Code of Toast.

Depending on the bread used, most of us have a very particular preference for levels of 'doneness'. These days all manner of hi-tech toasters are available, some with conveyor belts, some of which claim to 'read' the colour of the toast with a photocell, some with simple timers… but most of us can't resist intervening. Every toaster requires constant, neurotic jockeying, frequent checks on 'brownness' if horrible breakfast disappointment is to be avoided.

And what disappointment it can be. Who amongst us has never burned the toast? Who has not allowed the last piece of bread in the house to be catastrophically carbonised… the doomed attempt to 'scrape off the burned bits' and the whole day, subtly, but appreciably thrown into a sense of sadness and failure.

There is similar partisan passion concerning the serving temperature. Some believe the toast should be brought to the table at a temperature that sears the fingertips, all the better to melt the butter and absorb it. Others – otherwise sensible people, whose judgement in most matters is usually to be trusted – want their toast cold so that great curling waves of butter can be piled onto the surface without melting.

It's here that the toast rack comes into play: toast-making, like any great art form, is a matter of balancing like an acrobat on the precipice of disaster.

Toasting bread is unlike any other form of cooking. For the perfect finish, the toast must be warm, moist and steaming on the inside, crisp and dry on the outside. If toast is allowed to cool flat on a plate or breadboard, the steam in the centre is trapped and causes the crust to become unappealingly soft. There is nothing as disheartening as soggy toast. The toast rack is, therefore, the only tool by which one can allow the toast to cool in freely circulating air, allowing the steam to escape and retaining crispness.

That crisp surface is the result of the 'Maillard reaction', a process of non-enzymatic browning, caramelisation and finally pyrolisis... a very posh way of saying 'crisp and delicious'.

This also explains why you can't make toast in an oven or microwave. You need something that can hold the bread in place while intense heat is applied to the surfaces. An electric toaster is ideal; searing in a hot, dry pan is a good substitute, but best of all is a toasting fork and a fire.

Toast is the most elemental of foods, simple yet complex, utterly plain yet deserving of infinite tweaks and enhancements. Toast can be reassuringly humble or very, very posh.

Now.... what shall we put on it?

TYPES OF BREAD
★
FOR TOASTING

Bagels
Bagels are made from a slightly sweetened yeast dough which is poached in boiling water for a short time before baking. This sets a tough, elastic crust which keeps the texture of the bagel tight and firm. Bagels toast well, particularly when a little stale.

Baguette
A good baguette is already extremely crisp-crusted so toasting can make it laceratingly sharp. That said, the open, airy crumb texture means that baguette toast has a great affinity for anything that benefits from 'soaking up'.

Bloomer (Crusty White or Brown)
Bloomer is a British name for a hand-shaped crusty white or brown loaf. It's cooked directly on the oven floor and relies on an elastic crust to hold its distinctive 'cushion' shape. Taste can vary but it's a popular general-purpose loaf with good texture and toasting qualities.

Brioche
A French yeast bread, enriched with butter, milk and eggs – the latter of which give it a lovely yellow colour. Brioche makes a fluffy, light toast with a pronounced sweetness, so it works well with jams and preserves but also, strangely, with pâtés and foie gras.

Challah
Challah is a traditional Jewish bread, usually made in a braided pattern. It tastes a lot like brioche and toasts in the same way, but it is 'parve' (the neutral category in Kosher foods) so contains no dairy products.

Ciabatta
Ciabatta conjures up images of a centuries-old Italian tradition but in fact it was invented in 1982 specifically for sandwich making. The flavour is mild, the texture open and the crust soft. It toasts up a treat.

Cornbread

Good cornbread has a fudgy, cake-like consistency and is made with ground cornmeal instead of flour. Baking powder is used as a raising agent which means that a slight saltiness tempers the sweetness of the corn. Cornbread is difficult to brown and crisp but that hardly matters as it's so delicious in its naked state.

Corn Tortilla

Corn tortillas are clearly not toast at all, but they make a fantastic base for toppings of all kinds. Made with finely ground cornmeal, they can be loaded up with Mexican-inspired ingredients, and once fried or toasted retain their crunch well.

Farmhouse

'Farmhouse' generally indicates a more rustic loaf. Expect a tougher crust, perhaps a less regular crumb texture, but a more robust and yeasty flavour. If the bread is very moist and fresh, slice it and allow it to stand in the toaster (switched off) for an hour or two, which will dry it out a little.

Flatbread

A whole family of unleavened or lightly leavened breads from all corners of the globe. Flatbread is made by stretching out the dough on a griddle or slapping it onto the walls of the oven. As it has a closed, unaerated texture, it becomes crisp and brittle with toasting.

Granary

'Granary' flour is a product of the Hovis company, made by malting the basic grain, crushing and roasting before adding to brown flour and baking. It produces a dark, complex-flavoured loaf with good moisture, excellent keeping properties and the malt gives a smoky sweetness. Granary toasts well and is sturdy enough to stand up to weighty toppings.

Pan Pugliese

Pan pugliese is one of dozens of regional types of basic Italian rustic bread. It's made with white flour and olive oil but is salted much less than many breads. It's particularly good when stale and toasted in a lightly oiled frying pan.

Pumpernickel

Pumpernickel is a sourdough bread made from rye meal and grains. It's cooked for up to 24 hours at a low temperature, giving it an earthy, almost chocolatey, flavour and a dense, fudgy texture. Even when stale, pumpernickel won't make very crisp toast, but its depth of flavour makes this forgiveable.

Rye

Rye bread is made with varying proportions of rye flour which makes it denser and usually more brown in colour. It contains more dietary fibre than white breads and has a lower glycemic index (GI), making it so healthy your doctor will probably prescribe it.

Sandwich Loaf

Sandwich loaf (or, if you want to be really posh, 'pain de mie') is any white bread cooked in a square section tin, with soft crumb structure and good keeping properties. Most packaged 'white sliced' in the UK would qualify. As the name suggests, it's intended to make sandwiches that will stay appetising for as long as possible on the plate. This moistness means it may be hard to toast, so you could dry slices a little in a cool oven before toasting if you want it shatteringly crisp.

Soda Bread

Soda bread refers to any bread raised with baking soda rather than yeast. Soda breads can range from crumpet-like individual 'farls' to cakey Irish wheaten breads. Soda bread works extremely well with sharp cheeses and bacon.

Sourdough

Sourdough is bread that has been raised with a natural ferment rather than commercial yeast. It has an elastic crumb texture and a slight sourness, most noticeable in the crust, from the lactic acid created during fermentation. Fresh sourdough is moist and takes ages to crisp in the toaster, but if allowed to stale a little it makes some of the most exceptional toast you'll ever eat.

Spelt

Spelt is a species of wheat. It happens to be a very ancient one and has quite a few positive health benefits over some modern varieties. The spelt grain can be treated in exactly the same way as regular wheat, so almost any type of bread can be made with spelt. In toasting terms, spelt breads behave in exactly the same way as their non-spelt counterparts.

Walnut

One of a variety of nut breads, walnut benefits from toasting as the nuts take on a lovely smokiness. It's quite sweet so particularly good with sharp or salty cheeses.

Wholemeal

As the name implies, wholemeal flour uses more or less the whole of the grain, including parts of the oily 'germ' and the fibrous 'husk'. Many types of bread can be made from it but they will be brown, nutty, usually coarse-textured and less risen than white or 'refined'-flour loaves. Toasting brings out the nuttiness of wholemeal.

Pumpernickel

White Sourdough

Brioche

Flatbread

Baguette

Spelt

Farmhouse

Ciabatta

Walnut

Granary/Malted

Challah

Rye

Poppy Seed Bloomer

Brown Bloomer

Soda Bread

Pan Pugliese

Sandwich Loaf

Bagel

Cornbread

Corn Tortilla

Seeded

Wholemeal

BREAKFAST

★

TOASTS

PISTACHIO
★
DUKKAH & AVOCADO

Dukkah is an Egyptian topping made of chopped nuts, seeds
and herbs. This makes a lot more dukkah than you'll need
for the recipe. Store the remainder in an airtight container
and use to sprinkle over salads or grilled meats.

SERVES 2

TAKES 10 minutes

50g/2oz pistachios
1 tbsp sesame seeds
1 tbsp pumpkin seeds
2 tsp coriander seeds
2 tsp cumin seeds
1 tsp fennel seeds
1 tsp sweet smoked paprika
2 slices spelt or rye bread
1 ripe avocado
drizzle of extra virgin olive oil
few parsley stalks
flaky sea salt

Make the dukkah. Toast the pistachios, sesame
seeds and pumpkin seeds together in a dry frying
pan until golden brown, then tip into a spice
grinder or mini food processor. Add the coriander,
cumin and fennel seeds to the pan and toast until
fragrant. Tip into the grinder and add the paprika
and some sea salt flakes. Blitz briefly so that
everything is combined but the dukkah still has
a bit of texture.

Toast the bread. Halve the avocado and remove the
stone. Peel and cut into thin wedges. Drizzle with
a little olive oil and sprinkle each toast with 2–3
teaspoons of the dukkah and some parsley.

TOASTED BAGEL

★

LOX & CREAM CHEESE

A bagel with smoked salmon and cream cheese is a staple
of US diners and New York delis. Chopped red onions and
capers are the favoured accompaniments, sometimes
referred to in Yiddish as 'The Whole Schmeer'.

SERVES 4

TAKES 15 minutes, plus
at least 24 hours' curing

100g/4oz flaky sea salt
175g/6oz light brown muscovado
    sugar
500g/1lb 2oz skinless and boneless
    salmon fillet
4 bagels
200g/7oz cream cheese
1 very small red onion, finely
    chopped
2 tbsp capers
handful dill sprigs, chopped
1 lemon, cut into quarters
    (optional)
freshly ground black pepper

Line a lipped dish or baking tray with cling film, so
that it comes over the sides. Mix together the salt
and sugar, then sprinkle a third over the base of the
lined tray. Top with the salmon, then tip over the
remaining salt and sugar mix, pressing it into the
salmon. Fold the overhanging cling film over the
salmon and wrap well. Pop another tray or plate on
top of the salmon and weigh it down with some
heavy tins. Place in the fridge and leave to cure for
at least 24 hours, and up to four days.

Remove the salmon from the fridge, unwrap and
rinse under cold water to remove the salt and
sugar, then pat dry. Slice the bagels in half, toast
and then leave to cool a little. Generously spread
one side with the cream cheese. Thinly slice the
cured salmon and pile several slices on top of the
cream cheese (or drape over shop-bought smoked
salmon, if using). Scatter over the onion, capers
and dill. Add a squeeze of lemon juice, if liked, and
a grinding of black pepper, before topping with
the other half of the bagel. Any remaining cured
salmon will keep in the fridge for up to one week
wrapped in cling film.

BACON SOLDIERS

★

SOFT-BOILED EGG

Boiled eggs and 'dippy soldiers' are a childhood favourite that could surely never be improved upon... well, actually, almost anything can be made more gorgeous with the magical addition of bacon. Bacon butter can be made ahead of time and kept refrigerated.

SERVES 2

TAKES 10 minutes

2 rashers smoked streaky bacon
2 eggs
25g/1oz butter, softened
2 slices white farmhouse or
   granary bread
freshly ground black pepper

Bring a pan of water to the boil and heat the grill. Cook the bacon on a foil-lined tray under the grill, turning once, until really crispy. Remove and set aside to cool.

Carefully lower the eggs into the pan of boiling water, set the timer and simmer for 5½ minutes.

Meanwhile, finely chop the cooled bacon. Mash the butter in a bowl and stir through the bacon bits and some black pepper. Pop the bread under the grill and toast both sides, then spread with the bacon butter whilst warm and cut into soldiers.

Once the eggs are ready, lift them out of the water into egg cups and serve with the soldiers.

HUEVOS
★
RANCHEROS

It would be a pretty sophisticated cowpoke who could rustle up huevos rancheros over a campfire but the spirit of the Wild West makes this a terrific start to the day.

SERVES 4

TAKES 25 minutes

125g/4½oz cooking chorizo, diced
1 red onion, finely sliced
2 garlic cloves, crushed
400g/14oz tin cherry tomatoes
1 tbsp sliced jalapeños from a jar, finely chopped
1 tsp smoked paprika
2 tsp red wine vinegar
4 tbsp sunflower oil
400g/14oz tin black beans, drained and rinsed
4 small flour tortillas
4 eggs
1 ripe avocado
large handful coriander (cilantro)
4 tbsp soured cream (optional)
salt and freshly ground black pepper

Preheat the oven to 180°C fan/350°F/gas 6. Place a frying pan over medium heat and cook the chorizo for 5 minutes or until it has released its oil and begun to crisp up. Remove using a slotted spoon and set aside. Place the pan back on the heat, add the sliced onion and cook for 5 minutes until softened. Add 1 crushed garlic clove and cook for 30 seconds, then tip in the tomatoes, jalapeños, smoked paprika and vinegar. Season, bring to a simmer and cook gently for about 8 minutes, until thickened and reduced. Stir through the cooked chorizo and set aside.

In a separate pan, heat 1½ tbsp of the oil until really hot, tip in the beans and fry for 5 minutes over a high heat. Stir through the remaining garlic and cook for a further minute. Sprinkle with salt and set aside. Use 1½ tbsp of the oil to brush the tortillas on both sides. Place in a single layer on a baking tray and bake for 6–8 minutes or until crisp.

Heat the remaining oil in a frying pan and fry the eggs. Top the tortillas with a few spoonfuls of the tomato sauce, the beans and a fried egg. Halve the avocado and remove the stone, then scoop out the flesh and cut into thin wedges. Divide between the tortillas, and finish with sprigs of coriander. Serve some cooling soured cream alongside, if you like.

FULL ENGLISH
★
ON TOAST

The beauty of the classic full English is that it's infinitely variable. Mix and match the ingredients for a different 'fry-up' combo every time.

🍴 SERVES 4

⏰ TAKES 30 minutes

4 chipolata sausages (or any small sausage)
4 rashers smoked streaky bacon
8 cherry tomatoes
1 tbsp olive oil
200g/7oz button mushrooms, halved or quartered if large
1 garlic clove, crushed
few sprigs rosemary, leaves picked and finely chopped
large knob butter, plus extra for spreading
5 eggs
½ baguette
salt and freshly ground black pepper

Preheat the oven to 180°C fan/350°F/gas 6. Place the sausages on a lipped baking tray and cook in the oven for 8 minutes. Add the bacon rashers and return to the oven for 15–20 minutes, turning once, until the sausages are browned and the bacon is crisp (make sure you keep an eye on the bacon so that it doesn't burn). Add the tomatoes to the tray for the final 6 minutes, shaking the tray so that they are coated in the bacon fat.

Meanwhile heat the oil in a frying pan, throw in the mushrooms, season and cook for 5–8 minutes until softened. Add the garlic and rosemary to the pan, stir and cook for a further minute.

For the scrambled eggs, heat the butter in a frying pan. Crack the eggs into a jug, season and beat lightly with a fork. Pour into the pan and cook gently, stirring, until the eggs are just set but still creamy. Set aside.

Halve the baguette lengthways and widthways so that you have four pieces. Toast the bread and then butter well. Spoon the scrambled eggs over the toast, top with the mushrooms, a slice of bacon, a sausage and a couple of roasted tomatoes.

TURKISH EGGS
★
ON TOAST

Turkish dried chilli flakes are mild in heat but wonderfully fragrant. They keep for ages so it's worth grabbing a bag for the larder any time you pass a Turkish deli.

🍴 SERVES 2

⏰ TAKES 10 minutes

150g/5½oz Greek-style yoghurt
½ very small garlic clove, crushed
2 large slices poppy seed bloomer
35g/1½oz butter
2 eggs
1 heaped tsp Aleppo or Turkish chilli (hot pepper) flakes
6 small sage leaves
flaky sea salt

Bring a pan of water to the boil then turn down to a simmer. Meanwhile, spoon the yoghurt into a bowl, add the crushed garlic and plenty of salt and beat together well. Toast the bread.

Melt the butter in a small frying pan. While the butter is melting, crack the eggs into two separate cups. Using a slotted spoon gently swirl the simmering water. Carefully drop in the eggs and poach for 2–3 minutes. Once the butter has started to foam, stir in the chilli flakes then add the sage leaves and let them sizzle for 30 seconds or so.

Drizzle a little of the butter over each slice of toast. Spoon the yoghurt on top, making a dip with the back of a spoon. Lift the eggs out of the water using a slotted spoon and drain, then place into the dip in the yoghurt. Drizzle over the chilli and sage butter and eat straight away.

PA AMB

★

TOMÀQUET

A simple Spanish breakfast that can also do service as a sophisticated 'tapa'. Beware though: raw garlic is ferociously peppery. You might want to avoid too much kissing before heading to work.

SERVES 4

TAKES 5 minutes

8 slices sourdough bread, baguette or ciabatta
2 garlic cloves, halved
4 ripe and juicy tomatoes
extra virgin olive oil, to drizzle
slices of serrano or Ibérico ham (optional)
thin slices Manchego (optional)
flaky sea salt

Toast the bread, then whilst still warm lightly rub each slice with a cut side of the garlic. Halve the tomatoes and rub each slice of toast with one half, so that most of the insides of the tomato are on the bread and you are left with the skin. Drizzle generously with oil and sprinkle with a little sea salt. Top with the slices of ham and some Manchego cheese if you like, or enjoy just as it is.

EGG

★

IN THE HOLE

Kids the world over have delighted in coining names for this
simple breakfast. 'One-eyed Jack', 'Moon Egg' or 'Hen-in-
the-nest' are just a few. Remember to keep the yolk soft so
you can cut round the edges and dip in.

SERVES 1

TAKES 8 minutes

1 slice white farmhouse bread
large knob butter
1 egg
dollop tomato ketchup
salt and freshly ground black
    pepper

Using a 7cm/2½ inch round pastry cutter or glass,
stamp out a hole in the middle of the bread and
remove.

Heat half the butter in a frying pan over a gentle
heat. Once foaming, pop in the slice of bread and
bread disc and cook for 2–3 minutes until golden
brown. Flip the bread over and add the remaining
butter to the pan. Crack the egg into the hole of
the bread and cook for about 3 minutes, or until
the egg is set, covering with a lid for the final
minute. Transfer to a plate, grind over some black
pepper and sprinkle with salt. Serve with the bread
disc for dipping and a dollop of ketchup.

SCRAMBLED EGGS

★

PIPERADE

Piperade is a rich Basque stew of peppers and tomatoes. If you can find the authentic 'espelette' pepper of the region then it has a lovely fragrance. If you like, you can pep up your piperade by serving it with a slug of hot chilli sauce.

SERVES 4

TAKES 30 minutes

4 slices Bayonne ham or prosciutto
3 tbsp olive oil
2 (bell) peppers, a mixture of red and yellow, finely sliced
1 garlic clove, crushed
150g/5½oz tomatoes, roughly chopped
5 spring onions (scallions), finely sliced
4 slices seeded or granary bread
8 eggs
softened butter, for spreading
salt and freshly ground black or espelette pepper

Heat a large frying pan and cook the ham over a medium-high heat, without adding any oil, until really crisp on both sides. Remove from the pan and set aside. Pour the oil into the same pan, throw in the peppers and cook for about 6 minutes until softened. Add the garlic, stir well, then tip in the tomatoes. Cook for 5 minutes or until the tomatoes have softened and most of the juices have evaporated. Season and stir in the spring onions.

Meanwhile toast the bread. Crack the eggs into a jug, season and lightly beat. Push the vegetables to the side of the pan and pour in the eggs. Cook gently, stirring as you would for scrambled eggs until beginning to set but still creamy. Stir through the vegetables and leave to rest in the pan for 1 minute. Butter the toast and spoon over the scrambled eggs. Grind over some black or espelette pepper, then snap each slice of ham in half and place on top.

EGGS

★

BENEDICT

A favourite in posh hotel restaurants. The peak of the
Benedict experience is the way the yolk combines with
the hollandaise to bathe the bacon and soak the toast.
Even the strongest hangover can be banished by it.

🍴 SERVES 2

⏰ TAKES 20 minutes

2 egg yolks plus 2 whole eggs
100g/4oz cold butter, cubed, plus
   extra for spreading
1 tbsp lemon juice
6 rashers smoked streaky bacon
2 slices white farmhouse bread
salt and freshly ground black
   pepper

Bring a large pan of water to the boil and preheat
the grill.

To make the hollandaise, put the egg yolks, cold
butter and 1 tbsp of cold water into a pan. Set over
a very low heat and start whisking. The butter will
start to melt and the sauce will begin to thicken;
keep whisking continuously for 8–10 minutes. Once
you have a thick glossy sauce, remove from the
heat. Season and stir through the lemon juice, then
cover the pan and keep in a warm place.

Place the bacon on a foil-lined tray and grill until
crisp, turning once. Meanwhile, crack the two eggs
into separate cups. Using a slotted spoon, gently
swirl the simmering water and drop in the eggs.
Poach for 2–3 minutes, then remove using the
slotted spoon. While the eggs are cooking, toast
the bread and spread well with butter.

Top each slice of buttered toast with three rashers
of crisp bacon and a poached egg, then spoon
over the warm hollandaise and grind over some
black pepper.

EGGS
★
ROYALE

Give smoked salmon a few minutes out of the fridge to come to room temperature before using – this will ensure that the flavours and silky textures are at their best.

SERVES 2

TAKES 20 minutes

2 egg yolks plus 2 whole eggs
125g/4½oz cold butter, cubed,
   plus extra for spreading
1 tbsp lemon juice
100g/4oz spinach
2 slices spelt bread
85g/3oz smoked salmon
few parsley leaves, roughly
   chopped
salt and freshly ground black
   pepper

Bring a large pan of water to the boil and preheat the grill.

To make the hollandaise put the egg yolks, 100g/4oz of the cold butter and 1 tbsp cold water into a pan. Set over a very low heat and start whisking. The butter will start to melt and the sauce will begin to thicken; keep whisking continuously for 8–10 minutes. Once you have a thick glossy sauce, remove from the heat. Season and stir through the lemon juice, then cover the pan and keep in a warm place.

Crack the two eggs into separate cups. Using a slotted spoon, gently swirl the simmering water and drop in the eggs. Poach for 2–3 minutes, then remove using the slotted spoon.

While the eggs are poaching heat the remaining butter in a frying pan. Tip in the spinach, season and toss until just wilted. Toast the bread and spread well with butter.

Divide the spinach between the toast slices and top with the smoked salmon. Place a poached egg on top and spoon over the warm hollandaise. Finish with a scattering of chopped parsley.

EGGS

★

FLORENTINE

To make this veggie option really sing, take special care over cooking the spinach. It should be softly wilted. Don't be shy with the butter as, along with the nutmeg, it cuts through any 'chalkiness' in the spinach leaves.

SERVES 2

TAKES 20 minutes

2 egg yolks plus 2 whole eggs
125g/4½oz cold butter, cubed,
   plus extra for spreading
1 tbsp lemon juice
150g/5½oz spinach, tough stalks
   removed
freshly grated nutmeg
2 slices rye bread
few chives, finely chopped
salt and freshly ground black
   pepper

Bring a large pan of water to the boil and preheat the grill.

To make the hollandaise put the egg yolks, 100g/4oz of the cold butter and 1 tbsp cold water into a pan. Set over a very low heat and start whisking. The butter will start to melt and the sauce will begin to thicken; keep whisking continuously for 8 minutes. Once you have a thick glossy sauce, remove from the heat. Season and stir through the lemon juice, then cover the pan and keep in a warm place.

Crack the two eggs into separate cups. Using a slotted spoon, gently swirl the simmering water and drop in the eggs. Poach for 2–3 minutes, then remove using a slotted spoon. While the eggs are poaching, heat the remaining butter in a frying pan. Tip in the spinach, season and grate over some fresh nutmeg, then toss until just wilted. Toast the bread and spread well with butter.

Heap the wilted spinach onto the buttered toast then top with a poached egg. Spoon over the warm hollandaise and sprinkle with chopped chives.

SMOKED HADDOCK
★
SPINACH & QUAIL'S EGGS

Soft-boiled eggs in happy combination with rich smoked haddock are the principal flavours in a kedgeree, so spinach, tossed in a lightly curried butter, makes a harmonious background.

SERVES 4

TAKES 20 minutes

8 quail's eggs
400ml/14fl oz milk
1 bay leaf
6 peppercorns
1 onion, peeled and halved
385g/13½oz undyed smoked
   haddock
35g/1½oz butter, plus extra for
   spreading
1 tsp ground coriander
1 tsp garam masala
½ heaped tsp curry powder
300g/11oz spinach
4 slices wholemeal bread
salt and freshly ground black
   pepper

Bring a small pan of water to the boil. Lower the eggs into the water and simmer for 2½ minutes, then plunge into ice-cold water. Once cooled, gently peel off the shells.

In a separate pan, heat the milk, bay leaf, peppercorns and onion. Bring to a simmer then lower in the haddock – it should be submerged so add some hot water to top up the level if needed. Turn off the heat and leave it to poach for 8 minutes, then remove the fish.

Melt the butter in a large frying pan, add the spices and cook, stirring, for 2 minutes. Tip in the spinach, season, and stir until just wilted but still holding its shape.

Toast the bread, then butter well. Top with the spinach, then flake over some poached haddock, discarding the skin. Halve the quail's eggs and divide them between the toast slices, then grind over some black pepper.

ROASTED
★
SEED BUTTER

Peanuts are not actually nuts but seeds and contain large reserves of protein. Roasting and grinding produces a spreadable butter. You can do this with many types of seed and in this case the sweetish flavour of the sunflower seeds is enhanced with healthy agave syrup. A hint of salt brings out the sweetness.

MAKES 300g/11oz jar

TAKES 35 minutes

280g/10oz sunflower seeds
2 tbsp olive oil
1 tbsp agave syrup
4 slices brown bloomer
flaky sea salt

Preheat the oven to 160°C fan/315°F/gas 4. Tip the seeds onto a lipped baking tray and roast in the oven for 20–25 minutes or until a deep golden brown, shaking the tray every so often. Leave to cool a little, then tip into the bowl of a food processor.

Whizz until you have the consistency of butter – this may take up to 10 minutes – scraping the mixture down from the sides every so often. Add the oil and agave syrup, and a good few pinches of salt and blend. Check the level of sweetness and saltiness and adjust if necessary, then whizz again. Transfer to a jar and leave to cool completely. Toast the bread, then spread thickly with the seed butter.

The seed butter can be stored in the fridge, in an airtight jar, for up to two weeks.

SMOKED SALMON
★
BREAKFAST CUPS

Who said toast should be flat? Buttering the bread
on both sides and moulding into a muffin tin creates
little cases, half toasted, half deliciously fried, that
can contain anything. Here they make for a cracking
'breakfast on the go'.

🍴 SERVES 6

⏰ TAKES 35 minutes

6 slices white sandwich bread
75g/2½oz butter, melted
100g/4oz smoked salmon
2 tbsp double (heavy) cream
6 eggs
3 spears fine asparagus
freshly ground black pepper

Preheat the oven to 160°C fan/315°F/gas 4. Remove
the crusts from each slice of bread and brush both
sides with melted butter. Use the bread to line
6 holes of a muffin tin, pressing it down into the
tin well. Bake for 8–10 minutes until the bread has
crisped up a little, then remove from the oven.

Divide the smoked salmon between the toast cups,
making sure it covers the base and comes at least
halfway up the sides of the toast. Spoon 1 tsp of
the cream into each cup then crack in an egg. (If
your eggs are on the large side you may need to
discard some of the white before putting the egg
in the toast cup, but don't worry if it spills over
the edge a little.) Using a sharp knife, slice the
asparagus into thin ribbons and divide between the
cups, tucking them in around the eggs. Drizzle over
the remaining melted butter and bake for 15–20
minutes, depending how runny you like your eggs.

Remove from the oven and leave to cool for a few
moments, then use a knife to ease the cups from
the tin. Give the breakfast cups a good grind of
pepper before serving.

CHOCOLATE SPREAD
★
CREAM CHEESE

This recipe makes a large jar of chocolate spread.
You won't need it all but it will keep in the fridge for
up to two weeks.

SERVES 4

TAKES 30 minutes, plus cooling

250g/9oz hazelnuts
75g/2½oz dark chocolate, roughly chopped
75g/2½oz milk chocolate, roughly chopped
1 tbsp cocoa powder
75g/2½oz icing (confectioner's) sugar
1 tsp vanilla extract
pinch of salt
4 slices wholemeal bread
175g/6oz cream cheese

Preheat the oven to 160°C fan/315°F/gas 4. Tip the nuts onto a baking tray and roast in the oven for 15 minutes, shaking every so often, until golden brown. Leave to cool a little, then tip 200g/7oz of the roasted nuts into the bowl of a food processor.

Meanwhile, tip both chocolates into a bowl and melt over a pan of barely simmering water, then allow to cool.

Blend the nuts to a paste in the food processor. Sift in the cocoa powder and icing sugar, then add the cooled melted chocolate, vanilla extract and a good pinch of salt. Blend until smooth – about 10 minutes – scraping the mixture down from the sides every so often. Transfer to a jar, then leave to cool completely and firm up a little.

Toast the bread and spread thickly with the cream cheese. Top with several spoonfuls of chocolate spread, then roughly chop the remaining roasted hazelnuts and scatter these over the top.

FRENCH TOAST

★

BERRIES & MASCARPONE

Brioche is a sweet, egg-enriched bread, ideal for French
toast, and it marries well with cool, smooth cream cheese.
Such a rich and creamy base can take plenty of tartness
in the fruit compote so don't overdo the sugar.

SERVES 4

TAKES 25 minutes

6 slices brioche, halved diagonally
3 large eggs
100ml/3½fl oz milk
1 tsp vanilla bean paste or vanilla
  extract
½ tsp ground cinnamon
300g/11oz mixed berries such as
  blueberries, raspberries and
  blackberries
1 tbsp icing (confectioner's) sugar,
  plus extra to dust
50g/2oz butter
100g/4oz caster (granulated) sugar
4 tbsp mascarpone
4 tbsp maple syrup
pinch of salt

Lay the brioche slices on a tray. In a bowl, whisk
together the eggs, milk, vanilla bean paste,
cinnamon and a pinch of salt. Pour the mixture over
the bread slices and leave to soak for 5 minutes on
each side.

Meanwhile, tip half of the berries into a saucepan,
sprinkle over the 1 tbsp icing sugar and add a
splash of water. Set over a low heat and cook
for 4 minutes or until the berries have released
their juices. Use a fork to mash the softened
berries, then stir through the remaining berries
and set aside.

Place half the butter in a frying pan and set over a
medium heat. Sprinkle six of the soaked brioche
slices generously with caster sugar and flip, sugar-
side-down, into the frying pan. Cook for 2–3
minutes, or until golden brown. Sprinkle the other
side generously with caster sugar and flip over
again. Cook for a further 2–3 minutes. Repeat with
the remaining brioche slices. Pile three triangles of
French toast onto each plate, top with some of the
berry compote and a scoop of mascarpone. Drizzle
over the maple syrup, then dust with icing sugar.

BRIOCHE TOAST

★

PEACHES & CREAM

Supermarkets stock excellent ripe peaches but coating them in honey and baking until the edges scorch just seems to heighten and intensify all their flavour.

 SERVES 2

TAKES 25 minutes

2 large peaches or nectarines
2 tbsp runny honey
½ tbsp light brown muscovado
   sugar
4 slices brioche
butter for spreading
2 heaped tbsp clotted cream
1 heaped tbsp pistachios, roughly
   chopped

Heat the oven to 180°C fan/350°F/gas 6. Cut the peaches into quarters, removing the stone as you do. Place in a shallow baking tin lined with baking parchment. Drizzle with the honey and sprinkle over the sugar. Bake for 15–20 minutes or until softened and slightly tinged at the edges, then leave to cool a little.

Toast the bread then butter generously. Top with the peach quarters and drizzle over their cooking juices. Dollop on a spoonful of clotted cream, then scatter over the pistachios.

COCONUT CREAM
★
BANANAS & MAPLE PECANS

Everyone knows that a banana is a sensible and filling breakfast, but caramelising them elevates them to a whole new level. Make a few extra of the maple candied pecans too, as they make a wonderfully indulgent snack.

🍴 SERVES 2

⏰ TAKES 15 minutes, plus overnight chilling

400g/14oz tin coconut milk, minimum 70% coconut extract
25g/1oz coconut flakes
large knob butter, plus extra for spreading
1 tbsp caster (granulated) sugar
2 bananas
25g/1oz pecans
2 tbsp maple syrup
4 slices white farmhouse bread

The night before you want to make this, pop the whole tin of coconut milk in the fridge.

Put the coconut flakes into a frying pan and toast over a low heat, shaking every so often, until browned. Tip into a bowl and set aside.

Remove the coconut milk from the fridge. Scoop the firm coconut cream from the top of the tin and transfer this to a bowl. Using hand-held electric beaters, whip until smooth. Chill until ready to serve.

Melt the butter in the frying pan used to toast the coconut. Once foaming, sprinkle over the sugar and cook until golden and the sugar melted. Add the bananas and pecans then cook until the bananas are starting to caramelise, but haven't lost their shape, turning once. Pour over the maple syrup and let it bubble for 1–2 minutes.

Meanwhile, toast the bread, spread with butter and halve each slice diagonally. Top with the banana, pecans and maple sauce. Dollop over the coconut sauce and scatter with coconut flakes.

LUNCH

★

TOASTS

ESCALIVADA

★

TUNA

Escalivada is just the Catalan name for roasted vegetables.
The charred veg are made ahead of time and stored in a
marinade that takes on the flavours and soaks wonderfully
into toast. Albacore or ventresca tuna are a luxurious treat
but this is still wonderful made with regular tuna.

SERVES 4

TAKES 30 minutes

2 red onions
2 large (bell) peppers, a mixture of
   red and yellow, peeled
1 small aubergine (eggplant)
225g/8oz jar albacore tuna in extra
   virgin olive oil
10 cherry tomatoes
1 small garlic clove, crushed
1 tbsp red wine vinegar
4 slices pain de campagne
salt and freshly ground black
   pepper

Heat the grill to its highest setting. Cut the onions
into chunky wedges. Halve the peppers, remove
the seeds and cut into thick strips. Halve the
aubergine widthways and slice each half into long
wedges. Tip the vegetables onto a large baking
tray lined with foil. Drain the oil from the tuna and
spoon 2 tbsp of the oil over the vegetables. Season
and toss together, then spread out into an even
layer. Grill for 10–15 minutes, or until nicely charred.
Keep an eye on them so that they don't burn,
and turn the vegetables every so often. Add the
tomatoes to the tray for the final 4 minutes.

While the vegetables are cooking, make the
dressing. Combine the garlic, the reserved oil,
the vinegar and some seasoning in a jar, and shake
well. Transfer the vegetables to a large bowl, pour
over the dressing and toss to combine. Set aside
for a few minutes to cool and let the flavours
meld together.

Toast the bread. Pile the vegetables onto the toast
and top with chunks of tuna.

MOZZARELLA &

★

KALE PESTO

We all know kale is healthy... who guessed it could be tasty too? The secret here is whizzing the kale into a powerful herby pesto, then contrasting it with soft lumps of creamy buffalo mozzarella.

SERVES 4

TAKES 15 minutes

75g/3oz kale leaves, weight after tough stalks removed
½ fat garlic clove, finely chopped
zest ½ lemon and squeeze of juice
25g/1oz Parmesan, finely grated
25g/1oz pine nuts, toasted
85ml/3fl oz rapeseed (canola) oil
1 small ciabatta loaf
2 x 125g/4½oz balls buffalo mozzarella
salt and freshly ground black pepper

Bring a large pan of water to the boil, drop in the kale and blanch for 2 minutes. Drain and run under cold water, then squeeze out the excess water. Tip the kale into a food processor or mortar and pestle. Add the garlic, lemon zest, Parmesan, pine nuts and some seasoning, then whizz or pound to a rough paste. Slowly add the rapeseed oil followed by a squeeze of lemon juice. Taste and add a little more if needed.

Heat a griddle pan until really hot. Slice the ciabatta in half lengthways, then in half again so that you have four pieces. Pop onto the griddle, cut-side down, and cook until toasted and charred, then turn and toast the other side. Dollop a spoonful of pesto onto each slice of bread. Tear the mozzarella into chunks and divide among the ciabatta, then spoon over a little more pesto and grind over some black pepper.

You can store any leftover pesto in the fridge for up to two weeks – just make sure the surface is covered with oil.

AVOCADO & TAHINI
★
TOASTED CHICKPEAS

A good ripe avocado is as rich and voluptuous as a thick smearing of butter but a lot better for you. Here, that creamy texture is tweaked with cumin and tahini and imbued with a magical crunch by the cheeky sprinkling of toasted chickpeas.

SERVES 4

TAKES 25 minutes

210g/8oz tin chickpeas, rinsed
   and drained
1 tbsp olive oil
¼ tsp ground cumin
¼ tsp smoked paprika
few pinches allspice
2 tbsp tahini
1 tbsp lemon juice
4 slices seeded or rye bread
2 ripe avocados, peeled, stone
   removed, and sliced
½ small red onion, finely chopped
handful sprouted chia, radish or
   alfalfa
few sprigs dill, roughly chopped
salt and freshly ground black
   pepper

Preheat the oven to 180°C fan/350°F/gas 6. Use a clean tea towel to dry the chickpeas really well. Tip onto a lipped baking tray and bake for 10 minutes. Remove from the oven and drizzle with ½ tbsp of the oil. Scatter over the spices, season with salt and pepper and toss to coat. Return to the oven for 10 minutes, or until golden and crispy, giving them a shake halfway through.

Meanwhile, make the tahini dressing. In a bowl, combine the tahini, lemon juice, remaining oil, a little salt and 2–3 tbsp cold water, to make a fluid but not too runny dressing.

Toast the slices of bread. Spread a spoonful of the dressing over each slice of toast. Top with the avocado slices, a little red onion, the sprouts and toasted chickpeas. Drizzle over the remaining dressing and scatter over the dill.

WHITE BEAN
★
LEMON & SAGE PURÉE

White beans take to puréeing like few other ingredients and the smooth paste is an ideal vehicle for simple, clean flavours like lemon and sage. Such a virtuous blend could be served with a pork chop or as a hangover cure – possibly both at once – but it's definitely at its best on toast.

SERVES 2–4

TAKES 10 minutes

400g/14oz tin cannellini beans, rinsed and drained
zest and juice ½ lemon
3 tbsp Greek yoghurt
1 tbsp extra virgin olive oil, plus extra for frying
20 small sage leaves
½ baguette
salt and freshly ground black pepper

Place the drained beans into a bowl, and using a fork or potato masher crush to a rough paste (or just whizz them up in a mini food processor, making sure to reserve a few beans to mash in at the end for texture). Add most of the lemon zest and all the juice, the yoghurt, 1 tbsp extra virgin olive oil and season with salt and pepper. Finely chop a few sage leaves and add them to the beans, stir well.

Drizzle a little oil into a small frying pan and set over a medium heat. Add half the remaining sage leaves and fry for 30 seconds until dark green and crispy, watching to make sure they don't burn. Drain on kitchen paper and repeat with the rest of the leaves.

Heat the grill. Halve the baguette vertically, then again horizontally so that you have four pieces. Rub the cut surfaces of the baguette in the oil left in the sage pan, then pop under the grill to toast. Top the baguette with spoonfuls of the bean purée, the remaining lemon zest, a good grinding of black pepper, the crispy sage leaves and any remaining oil from the pan.

★

GOAT'S CHEESE TARTINE

A tartine is a French open sandwich. In this clever veggie version a dark, nutty bread is matched with a mild goat's cheese. Whisking the cheese is a cheffy trick that not only improves and lightens the texture but also looks extremely smart swirled onto the toast.

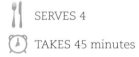

SERVES 4

TAKES 45 minutes

12 cherry tomatoes, halved
1 tsp brown sugar
1 tbsp olive oil
200g/7oz soft goat's cheese
splash of milk (optional)
handful thyme sprigs, leaves
    picked
4 slices walnut bread
2 handfuls baby salad leaves
salt and freshly ground black
    pepper

Preheat the oven to 160°C fan/315°F/gas 4 and line a roasting tray with baking parchment. Place the tomatoes, cut-side up, on the roasting tray. Sprinkle over the sugar and drizzle with the olive oil, season and roast for 35 – 40 minutes, until the tomatoes are starting to collapse. Leave to cool a little.

While the tomatoes are roasting, whisk the goat's cheese in a bowl with a splash or two of milk, if needed, until smooth, creamy and spreadable. Season with salt and pepper and stir through most of the thyme.

Toast the bread, then spread thickly with the goat's cheese. Top with a few baby leaves, the tomatoes and a drizzle of their roasting juices, then scatter over the remaining thyme.

MINT & WALNUT
★
BABA GANOUSH

Baba ganoush is a world away from the tired and oily aubergines of a thousand sad moussakas. The skin is scorched for a smoky note and the flesh, steamed in the skin, takes on a satiny texture. Toasted flatbreads or pitta make a toast base that's thinner but has a lovely chewiness.

SERVES 6

TAKES 50 minutes

3 aubergines (eggplant)
2 heaped tbsp tahini
juice ½ lemon
2 garlic cloves, crushed
2 tbsp olive oil, plus extra for
    drizzling
½ tsp chilli (hot pepper) flakes
    (use Aleppo or Turkish chilli
    flakes if available), plus a few
    extra pinches
large handful mint leaves, roughly
    chopped, plus a few extra leaves
6 pitta breads or small flatbreads
50g/2oz walnuts, toasted
salt and freshly ground black
    pepper

Prick the skin of the aubergines with a fork, then place directly over the flame of a gas hob. Cook until the skin is blackened and charred, and the flesh is very soft, using a pair of tongs to turn them every so often. This will take about 15 minutes. (You could char the aubergines under the grill, but this will take a little longer.) Remove the aubergines from the hob and leave to cool a little. Once cool enough to handle, peel off and discard the skin and pop the flesh into a sieve set over a bowl. Leave to drain and cool completely for 30 minutes.

Tip the aubergine flesh into a bowl and add the tahini, lemon juice, garlic, oil, chilli flakes and the mint. Season generously and stir to combine. Toast the pitta or flatbread, then spoon over the baba ganoush. Roughly chop the toasted walnuts and scatter these over the top. Sprinkle with some chilli flakes and mint leaves, and drizzle over a little oil.

BLUE CHEESE, FIGS

★

PARMA HAM

Ripe figs have a sweetness that borders on the indecent. Paired with the salt tang of the ham and the creamy body of the cheese they are sublime. Rye bread can sometimes feel unforgivingly virtuous but it hasn't the resolve to resist yielding to such a seductive topping.

SERVES 4

TAKES 25 minutes

10 baby figs
½ tsp demerara sugar
2 tsp runny honey
drizzle of extra virgin olive oil
4 slices rye bread
140g/5oz soft blue cheese, like St Agur or Roquefort, sliced
4 slices Parma ham
1 tbsp good-quality balsamic vinegar

Preheat the oven to 160°C fan/315°F/gas 4. Cut the figs in half through the stalk and place cut-side up onto a lipped baking tray lined with baking parchment. Sprinkle over the sugar, drizzle with the honey and oil, and roast for 20 minutes, until juicy and sticky.

Once the figs are ready, toast the bread then drizzle with some of the juices from the roasting tray. Top with the slices of blue cheese and Parma ham, then divide the figs between the toast. Drizzle over any remaining figgy juices and lastly the balsamic vinegar.

PINE NUTS
★
CATALAN SPINACH

The sweet and sour combination of honey and vinegar
is a Moorish influence on this Catalan speciality, but
it's the almost silken texture of the baby spinach that
really shines through. This is toast to toy with as the
sun goes down and the condensation forms on a
chilled glass of Manzanilla.

SERVES 2

TAKES 10 minutes

1 tbsp extra virgin olive oil, plus
   extra to drizzle
1 garlic clove, finely sliced
1 shallot, finely chopped
2 tbsp plump raisins
1 tbsp pine nuts
2 thick slices sourdough bread
160g/6oz baby spinach
splash of sherry vinegar
drizzle of runny honey
salt and freshly ground black
   pepper

Heat the oil in a large frying pan, add the garlic and
gently cook until browned, then remove using a
slotted spoon and discard. Add the shallot to the
pan and cook for about 5 minutes until softened,
then throw in the raisins and pine nuts and cook
for another few minutes.

Meanwhile, drizzle both sides of the bread with a
little oil and pop under the grill, or on a griddle pan,
and toast both sides.

Pile the spinach into the pan with the raisins and
pine nuts and toss until just beginning to wilt.
Season well, then add a splash of vinegar and
drizzle of honey. Stir together then spoon onto
the slices of hot toasted sourdough and drizzle
over a little extra oil.

SOFT-BOILED EGG
★
ASPARAGUS & PECORINO

Fresh young asparagus spears are a terrific treat when they come into season after a dull winter. Pecorino adds a salty tang and keeping the eggs soft boiled creates a creamy sauce without really trying.

SERVES 2

TAKES 15 minutes

2 medium eggs
2 slices poppy seed bloomer
12–16 fine asparagus spears,
   trimmed
1 tbsp extra virgin olive oil
15g/½oz pecorino
small handful basil leaves
salt and freshly ground black
   pepper

Bring a pan of water to the boil. Carefully lower in the eggs and set a timer for 6½ minutes. Once the time is up use a slotted spoon to remove the eggs and plunge into ice-cold water. Set aside.

Meanwhile, heat a griddle pan or the grill. Toast the bread on each side, then set aside on plates. Toss the asparagus in ½ tbsp of the oil and season. Griddle or grill for about 2 minutes, or until just tender and slightly charred, turning a few times. Peel the eggs and cut them in half lengthways.

Drizzle each slice of toast with the remaining oil. Divide the asparagus between the slices of toast, then top with the egg halves. Shave over the pecorino, scatter with basil leaves and grind over a little black pepper.

THYME-BUTTERED
★
MUSHROOMS

Cooking mushrooms drives off a lot of their water content, which means that the absorbent little devils can soak up all that gorgeous melted butter and the fragrance of the thyme. Don't waste a drop of the pan juices.

🍴 SERVES 1

⏰ TAKES 20 minutes

large knob butter, plus a little
    extra
1 shallot, finely sliced
140g/5oz mixed mushrooms,
    such as chestnut (cremini),
    portobello, shiitake or oyster
1 garlic clove, crushed
½ tsp green peppercorns in brine,
    drained and roughly chopped
    (optional)
2 lemon thyme sprigs, leaves
    picked, plus a few extra leaves
    to serve
1 slice white farmhouse bread
salt

Gently heat the knob of butter in a large frying pan. Once foaming, add the shallot and cook for 3–4 minutes, until softened, stirring every so often.

Cut the mushrooms in half, or quarters if they are large. Increase the heat and throw them into the pan, adding a little extra butter if needed. Cook, stirring for 8–10 minutes, until the mushrooms are softened and browning here and there but still holding their shape. Add the garlic and the peppercorns, if using, to the pan and cook for 2 minutes. Stir through the thyme leaves and season with salt.

Toast the bread then butter well, top with the mushrooms and their juices, and scatter over a few extra thyme leaves.

HAVARTI CHEESE

★

CHORIZO & RED PEPPERS

Havarti is a semi-soft Danish cheese with a lovely subtle
buttery flavour and a remarkable talent for melting.
The chorizo will give up its flavoured oil with almost no
persuasion at all and the two will meld in a way that's
frankly indecent.

🍴 SERVES 4

⏰ TAKES 30 minutes

2 red (bell) peppers
4 cooking chorizo sausages
drizzle of olive oil
4 slices olive bread
4 slices havarti
large handful lamb's lettuce
  or other salad leaves

Heat the grill to high. Quarter the peppers then
remove the seeds and any membrane. Pop under
the grill, skin-side up, and grill for about 15 minutes,
until the flesh has softened and the skin is blistered
and charred. Place the hot peppers in a bowl, cover
with cling film and set aside.

Cut the chorizo sausages at an angle into thick
slices. Heat the oil in a frying pan, add the sausage,
and fry, stirring, until cooked through and a little
crispy.

Meanwhile, lightly toast the bread, then top with
the havarti and pop under the grill until melted and
bubbling. Peel the skin from the cooled peppers
and slice into chunky strips. Top the melted cheese
with the peppers, chorizo and some leaves.

WHIPPED GORGONZOLA

★

ROCKET & HONEY DRIZZLE

Whipping cheese with crème fraîche makes for a delectably smooth topping, full of flavour but with the fat content reduced. The sweet honey forms a foil for the saltiness of the Gorgonzola.

SERVES 2

TAKES 10 minutes

85g/3oz Gorgonzola Dolce
3 tbsp crème fraîche
2 slices spelt, rye or wholewheat
   bread
2 small handfuls rocket (arugula)
   leaves
1–2 tbsp runny honey
salt and freshly ground black
   pepper

Place the Gorgonzola in the bowl of a food processor, or in a small bowl, along with the crème fraîche and some seasoning. Whizz or beat with hand-held electric beaters until smooth and creamy, scraping the mixture down from the sides every so often.

Toast the bread until crisp and spread thickly with the whipped Gorgonzola. Top with the rocket, then drizzle generously with honey.

CHIPOTLE PRAWNS & CORN
★
AVOCADO CREME TOSTADA

This might well be the most enjoyable combination of foods available for such a low carbohydrate intake.

SERVES 4

TAKES 30 minutes

20 raw king prawns (jumbo shrimp), shelled and deveined
2 tsp chipotle paste
1½ tbsp sunflower oil
1 sweetcorn cob
4 soft corn tortillas
2 ripe avocados
1 lime
small bunch coriander (cilantro), leaves picked
4 spring onions (scallions), finely sliced on the diagonal
salt and freshly ground black pepper

In a bowl, toss the prawns with the chipotle paste along with 1 tsp of the oil. Set aside to marinate.

Preheat the oven to 180°C fan/350°F/gas 6. Heat the grill or a griddle pan to high. Brush the corn with 1 tsp of the oil and season. Griddle or grill for 10 – 15 minutes until cooked through and slightly charred, turning the cob regularly. Set aside.

Brush the corn tortillas on both sides with the remaining oil and place in a single layer on a baking tray. Bake for 6 – 8 minutes or until crisp.

Halve the avocados, remove the stone and peel. Roughly chop and place in a food processor or blender. Grate in most of the lime zest and squeeze in all of the juice, then season. Whizz until smooth (add a drop of cold water for a smoother texture).

Hold the cooled corn vertically on a chopping board and cut off the kernels.

Reheat the griddle or grill and cook the prawns for 2 minutes or until cooked through, turning once.

Spoon avocado creme onto each tortilla, spreading it out. Top with the corn, prawns and a handful of coriander leaves. Scatter over the spring onions and grate over a little more lime zest, then spoon over the remaining avocado creme.

WALNUT BRITTLE

★

ROASTED GRAPES & RICOTTA

Roasting grapes dries them to a fudgy texture and concentrates their sweetness. Make plenty of the walnut brittle as you'll be helping yourself to it from the jar for days to come.

SERVES 4

TAKES 25 minutes

225g/8oz black grapes
1½ tbsp extra virgin olive oil
½ tbsp balsamic vinegar
50g/2oz walnuts
2 tbsp brown sugar
½ tbsp honey
1 rosemary sprig, leaves picked and finely chopped
250g/9oz good-quality ricotta
4 slices sourdough bread
salt and freshly ground black pepper

Heat oven to 180°C fan/350°F/gas 6. Toss the grapes with 2 tsp of the oil, the balsamic vinegar and some seasoning. Transfer to a tray lined with baking parchment and roast for 15–20 minutes, until sticky and syrupy. Leave to cool a little.

Meanwhile toast the walnuts in a hot frying pan until golden. Stir in 1 tsp of the oil, the sugar, honey, rosemary leaves and a good few pinches of salt. Let it bubble gently for about 3 minutes, until the sugar has caramelised. Tip onto a tray and leave to cool completely.

Place the ricotta into a small bowl and beat well. Add a good few pinches of salt and pepper and the remaining oil and continue to beat until smooth but spreadable.

Toast the bread and leave to cool briefly, then spread with the ricotta. Top with the grapes and their sticky juices. Chop or bash the walnut brittle into smaller pieces and scatter over the toast.

COURGETTES, CHILLI
★
MINT & FETA

Cooked courgettes can be mushy and disappointing, but using them raw and marinated like this turns them into something completely different. A stunningly crisp and sparkling salad in which to bury nuggets of salty feta.

SERVES 4

TAKES 15 minutes

1 large or 2 small courgettes
  (zucchini)
1½ tbsp extra virgin olive oil
few good pinches chilli (hot
  pepper) flakes, plus extra to
  serve
small handful mint leaves,
  roughly chopped
zest ½ lemon
4 slices pane pugliese or other
  rustic bread
140g/5oz feta, broken into large
  chunks
salt and freshly ground black
  pepper

Slice the courgette lengthways into thin ribbons using a vegetable peeler or mandoline. Place in a bowl and toss through 1 tbsp of the oil, the chilli flakes, most of the mint, lemon zest and some seasoning. Set aside to soften for 5 minutes.

Toast the bread and drizzle with the remaining oil. Top with the courgette ribbons and crumble over the feta, then sprinkle over a little extra chilli and the remaining mint.

HALLOUMI &

★

HARISSA DRESSING

Plain harissa is a Moroccan spice paste of astonishing hotness. As part of a dressing, it has a chance to show off its warmth and fragrance. Halloumi, which can sometimes seem uninspiringly plain, just begs to be dressed this way.

🍴 SERVES 4

⏰ TAKES 15 minutes

1½ tsp harissa (use rose harissa
  if you can find it)
1 garlic clove, crushed
zest and juice ½ lemon
2 tsp honey
2 tbsp extra virgin olive oil
1 heaped tbsp pumpkin seeds
4 slices seeded bread
250g/9oz halloumi
4 handfuls salad leaves
salt and freshly ground black
  pepper

To make the dressing, put the harissa, garlic, lemon zest and juice, honey and oil in a jam jar, season, pop on the lid and shake for 30 seconds.

Heat a frying pan over a medium-high heat. Tip the pumpkin seeds into the pan and toast until they begin to pop, shaking the pan every so often. Transfer to a bowl and set aside. Toast the bread.

Return the frying pan to a medium heat. Cut the halloumi into 8 or 12 slices, then place in the hot pan and cook for 1–2 minutes on each side, or until softened and golden brown.

Top the slices of toast with a little of the dressing, the salad leaves and the warm halloumi slices. Drizzle over some more of the dressing and scatter over the pumpkin seeds.

Any remaining dressing can be stored in the fridge for up to a week.

CHARRED SPRING ONIONS
★
ROMESCO & PANCETTA

This dish was inspired by 'calçotada', a Spanish festival where diners tuck into grilled calçots – a type of spring onion – dipped into almond romesco sauce.

SERVES 4

TAKES 30 minutes

2 red (bell) peppers
2 tomatoes
2 garlic cloves
50g/2oz blanched hazelnuts
small bunch parsley, roughly
   chopped, including stalks
1½ tsp smoked paprika
1 tbsp sherry vinegar
½ baguette
3½ tbsp extra virgin olive oil
16 spring onions (scallions),
   trimmed
8 thin slices pancetta
salt and freshly ground black
   pepper

Heat the grill to high. Halve the peppers and remove the seeds and membrane. Place onto a baking tray, skin-side up, along with the tomatoes and garlic. Grill for about 15 minutes or until softened and skins blackened, turning the tomatoes halfway through. Place the vegetables in a bowl, cover with cling film and leave to cool.

Toast the hazelnuts in a small frying pan. Once the vegetables are cool, peel off the skins and place the flesh in a food processor. Add the hazelnuts, parsley, paprika, vinegar and some seasoning. Cut off a very thin slice from each end of the baguette and add these to the food processor. Whizz until almost smooth, then, with the motor still running, slowly add 3 tbsp of the oil and 1 tbsp cold water.

Toss the spring onions with the remaining oil and arrange on a foil-lined baking tray. Place under a hot grill for 2–3 minutes, or until softened and slightly charred. Grill the pancetta for 2 minutes, or until cooked and crisp, turning once.

Halve the baguette lengthways and widthways to make four pieces, then toast. Spread on some romesco sauce. Top with the spring onions, snapped pancetta and a grind of black pepper.

SNACK & CANAPÉ

★

TOASTS

FIG TAPENADE &

★

CRÈME FRAÎCHE CROSTINI

Kalamata olives have a smooth texture and a pleasant saltiness from brining. Combining them with sweet figs in a tapenade gives a lovely twist to this Provençal classic.

🍴 MAKES 12 crostini

⏰ TAKES 20 minutes

75g/2½oz dried figs, roughly chopped
125g/4½oz black kalamata olives, pitted
handful flat-leaf parsley, leaves picked
3 thyme sprigs, leaves picked, plus extra to serve
3 tbsp capers, drained and rinsed
½ garlic clove, finely chopped
3 tbsp good-quality extra virgin olive oil
squeeze lemon juice
12 thin slices rustic baguette
4 tbsp crème fraîche
salt and freshly ground black pepper

Put the dried figs into a bowl and cover with boiling water. Set aside to soak for 10 minutes, then drain and pat dry. Pop the figs, olives, parsley, thyme, capers, garlic, oil and lemon juice into the bowl of a food processor and whizz briefly to a paste. Season with salt and pepper.

Toast the slices of bread. Spread with the tapenade and dollop on a spoonful of crème fraîche. Top with a few extra thyme leaves to garnish.

BROAD BEAN, MINT &
★
GOAT'S CHEESE CROSTINI

Fresh broad beans are a world away from their canned or frozen brethren. Here, crushed to a rough paste and perked up with lemon juice, they make a healthy spread that sings of spring. Like peas, broad beans love mint.

🍴 MAKES 12 crostini

⏰ TAKES 25 minutes

350g/12oz podded broad (fava) beans, defrosted if frozen
zest ½ lemon and squeeze juice
2 tbsp extra virgin olive oil, plus extra to drizzle
handful mint leaves, roughly chopped
12 thin slices sourdough baguette
25g/1oz skin-on hazelnuts
85g/3oz ashed goat's cheese
handful red amaranth micro leaves (optional)
salt and freshly ground black pepper

Preheat the oven to 160°C fan/315°F/gas 4.

Bring a large pan of water to the boil. Drop the beans into the boiling water and simmer for 1–2 minutes, then plunge into ice-cold water. Drain and pop the broad beans out of their skins, then transfer to the bowl of a food processor. Add most of the lemon zest, the juice, oil and some seasoning, then whizz briefly to a chunky paste, or pop into a bowl and crush with a fork. Stir through the mint.

Drizzle the bread with a little oil and place on a baking tray. Pop the hazelnuts on a lipped baking tray and place both in the oven. Bake for 6–8 minutes until the bread is golden and crisp and the hazelnuts are golden brown. Leave the nuts to cool a little, then roughly chop them.

Spread the toasted slices with broad bean purée, then crumble over the goat's cheese and scatter with the toasted hazelnuts. Top with the remaining lemon zest and, if using, a few micro amaranth leaves.

BAKED CAMEMBERT

★

ROSEMARY & TRUFFLE OIL

Few things are as jaw-droppingly indulgent as a whole
cheese, baked to the point of collapsing surrender and
anointed with decadent truffle oil. To avoid the temptation
to lick it off your date's fingers, serve with small pieces of
toasted baguette to dip and smear.

SERVES 4–6

TAKES 30 minutes

250g/9oz Camembert, in a box
½ garlic clove, thinly sliced
few rosemary sprigs
2 tbsp white wine
1 tbsp runny honey
12–18 thin slices baguette
drizzle of truffle oil (optional)
freshly ground black pepper

Remove the cheese from the fridge 1 hour before
you want to cook it, so that it can come to room
temperature.

Preheat oven to 160°C fan/315°F/gas 4. Take the
cheese out of its box and unwrap. Sit the base of
the box inside the top and put the cheese back
into the box, then pop it onto a baking tray. Use
a sharp knife to make slits all over the top of the
cheese. Poke the garlic and rosemary into the
holes, pour over the wine and honey, then grind
over some black pepper. Bake for 20 minutes,
adding the slices of baguette to the baking tray
after 12 minutes.

Remove from the oven and leave the Camembert
to cool a little before drizzling with the truffle oil,
if using. Serve the toasted baguette slices alongside,
spreading them liberally with the melted cheese.

BRESAOLA WITH
★
FENNEL & APPLE

Here the fennel, celery and apple are made into a remoulade, a kind of super-posh coleslaw. The light fresh flavours balance the salty intensity of the dried beef.

MAKES 24 canapés

TAKES 20 minutes

1 small fennel bulb, quartered and core removed
1 celery stick and leaves
1 small apple
2 heaped tbsp mayonnaise
2 tbsp crème fraîche
2 tsp wholegrain mustard
handful parsley, finely chopped
24 small pieces seeded bread
6 slices bresaola, cut into small pieces
salt and freshly ground black pepper

Preheat the oven to 160°C fan/315°F/gas 4.

Make the remoulade. Slice the fennel very finely and place into a bowl. Set aside any celery leaves then finely slice the stick. Cut the apple into matchsticks and tip these, along with the celery, into the bowl.

In a separate bowl, combine the mayonnaise, crème fraîche, mustard, parsley and some seasoning. Spoon over the vegetables and apple and stir everything together.

Pop the pieces of bread on a baking tray and bake for about 10 minutes, or until crisp. Top the pieces of toast with a spoonful of the fennel and apple remoulade, pieces of bresaola and a few celery leaves.

PANZANELLA
★
BRUSCHETTA

The secret to a panzanella – Italian bread salad – is to salt
the tomatoes in advance so that they give up their juices,
which are then soaked up by the chunks of stale bread.
Here, the bread is replaced with oily, garlicky toast –
delicious and more portable.

MAKES 12 bruschetta

TAKES 35 minutes

350g/12oz red and yellow baby
   tomatoes
½ small red onion, finely sliced
12 slices pane pugliese
2 tbsp extra virgin olive oil, plus
   extra for drizzling
2 garlic cloves, halved
2 tsp capers, roughly chopped
2 tsp red wine vinegar
pinch sugar
handful basil leaves, large ones
   torn
salt and freshly ground black
   pepper

Halve or quarter the tomatoes. Tip them into a
bowl and sprinkle with a little salt. Place the sliced
onion in a bowl, sprinkle with a little salt and cover
with cold water. Set the tomatoes and onion aside
for 15 minutes.

Meanwhile, heat the oven to 160°C fan/315°F/gas 4.
Drizzle the slices of bread with a little oil and bake
for 6–8 minutes, until golden and crisp. Rub with
the cut side of the garlic.

Drain the tomatoes, reserving the juices, and tip
into a bowl. Drain the onions and add these to
the tomatoes, along with the capers. In another
bowl, whisk together 1 tbsp of the reserved tomato
juices, the vinegar, sugar and the oil. Season and
pour this over the tomatoes. Set aside for 15
minutes to let the flavours develop.

Stir through most of the basil then pile onto the
pieces of toast letting the juices soak through.
Scatter over the remaining basil before serving.

CONFIT

★

GARLIC

Garlic slow-poached in oil is a preserve but it won't last long in your storecupboard. It's far too good when smeared onto everything from vegetables to cheese. Do try it in its purest form first though, spread on toast.

 MAKES 12

TAKES 2 hours

3–4 garlic bulbs (at least 36 good-sized cloves)
2 rosemary sprigs
3 thyme sprigs
1 bay leaf
8 black peppercorns
2 strips lemon peel
250ml/9fl oz extra virgin olive oil, plus extra if needed
12 thin slices baguette or ciabatta
sea salt flakes

Separate the garlic bulbs into cloves. Peel each clove and put into a small saucepan. Add the rosemary, thyme, bay leaf, peppercorns, lemon peel and a little salt. Pour in the oil – the garlic needs to be completely submerged so top up with more oil if needed. Heat the oil until it is barely simmering, and cook over a very low heat, stirring now and then, for about 40 minutes or until a knife poked into a clove glides in easily. Remove from the heat and leave to cool completely in the pan. Pour the contents of the pan into a sterilised jar and use straight away or refrigerate for up to a month.

When ready to serve, toast the bread. Spoon about three garlic cloves onto each slice, and spread. Drizzle with a little of the oil from the jar and sprinkle over some sea salt flakes.

PEPPERED STEAK

★

TAGLIATA CROSTINI

Good tagliata should be as rare as you can bear and positively dripping with juices. Even more so here, where the crostini will soak up everything so that none of that gorgeous flavour goes to waste.

MAKES 12 crostini

TAKES 15 minutes

12 slices ciabatta bread
225g/8oz thick sirloin steak
2½ tbsp extra virgin olive oil
1 tsp cracked black pepper
½ garlic clove, crushed
½ tbsp balsamic vinegar
handful rocket (arugula) leaves
small chunk Parmesan
salt

Heat a griddle pan over a high heat until really hot. Toast both sides of the bread on the griddle then set aside. Rub the steak all over with ½ tbsp of the oil and press the pepper into both sides. Cook the steak on the hot griddle for 2–3 minutes on each side, depending on the thickness. It should be nicely browned on the outside and pink in the middle. Remove and set aside to rest for 5 minutes.

Meanwhile, put the garlic into a small bowl. Sprinkle over a pinch of salt and mash to a paste. Stir in the vinegar and the remaining oil.

Thinly slice the steak. Top each slice of ciabatta with some rocket, a few strips of steak and a drizzle of the dressing, then shave over some Parmesan.

LEMON, PEAS &
★
SMOKED MACKEREL PÂTÉ

Smoked mackerel is so much of a supermarket staple these days that we rarely bother dressing it up. Blanched peas, however, pop in the mouth, giving a surprising fruity top-note to the smoky fish.

MAKES 24 canapés

TAKES 15 minutes

200g/7oz smoked mackerel
125g/4½oz full-fat cream cheese
3 tbsp Greek-style yoghurt
2 tbsp creamed horseradish
zest and juice ½ lemon
25g/1oz frozen peas
24 small slices soda bread
handful pea shoots
24 edible flowers, such as violas
   (optional)
salt and freshly ground black
   pepper

Bring a small pan of water to the boil. Remove the skin from the smoked mackerel, discard any bones, flake the flesh and set aside. In a bowl, beat the cream cheese, yoghurt, horseradish and lemon juice until smooth. Season with pepper and a little salt, then fold through the flaked mackerel.

Blanch the peas in a pan of boiling water for 2 minutes, then plunge into ice-cold water. Drain and set aside.

Heat the grill. Place the bread on a baking tray and toast both sides under the grill. Leave to cool, then top generously with the pâté. Scatter over the drained peas, some pea shoots, a little grated lemon zest and ground black pepper. Finally, top with an edible flower, if using.

WHIPPED
★
SALT COD CROSTINI

Salting and drying fish adds great depth to the flavour and whipping it up, as here, makes it light and fresh.

MAKES 12 crostini

TAKES 30 minutes, plus overnight soaking

250g/9oz salt cod
3 garlic cloves, 2 lightly bashed, 1 halved
few thyme sprigs
1 bay leaf
6 black peppercorns
2 strips lemon zest
500ml/17fl oz whole milk
125g/4½oz potatoes, peeled and diced
4 tbsp extra virgin olive oil
12 slices rustic baguette
handful micro leaf garlic chives

Start the day before: rinse the salt cod well then place in a bowl and cover with cold water. Chill for 24 hours, changing the water every so often.

Drain the cod and place in a saucepan. Add the 2 bashed garlic cloves, thyme, bay leaf, peppercorns and lemon zest to the pan, then pour over the milk. The cod should be completely submerged. Pop on the heat, bring to a simmer and let it cook for 5 minutes. Turn off the heat and set aside for a further 5 minutes. Lift the cod out of the milk and set aside. Place the pan back on the heat and add the potatoes. Bring to the boil and simmer for 8 minutes, or until tender. Set a sieve over a bowl and drain the potatoes, reserving the cooking liquid. Set aside the garlic but discard all the other aromatics.

Put the potatoes in a food processor. Peel off the skin from the cod and remove any bones, then flake the flesh into the food processor. Squeeze the garlic out of its skin, add this too and whizz everything to a paste. Pour in the olive oil and up to 2 tbsp of the milk then whizz until smooth – it should be a soft, spreadable consistency.

Toast the bread, then rub lightly with the cut side of the halved garlic whilst still warm. Leave to cool and spread generously with the whipped salt cod. Top with some micro garlic chives before serving.

★

CHICKEN LIVER PÂTÉ

Really, really posh toast would be brioche with foie gras smeared on it, but a well-made, buttery chicken liver parfait can be every bit as distinguished at about a tenth of the price.

🍴 MAKES 24 canapés

⏰ TAKES 1 hour 25 minutes

250g/9oz chicken livers
175g/6oz butter, diced
2 shallots, finely sliced
1 garlic, finely chopped
6 sage leaves, finely sliced, plus
   1 extra leaf
50ml/2fl oz port
50ml/2fl oz double (heavy) cream
freshly grated nutmeg
3 thick slices white bread
small handful micro leaves, such
   as rocket (arugula) or sorrel
salt and freshly ground black
   pepper

Rinse the livers, and use scissors to snip away any bits of sinew, then pat dry. Melt 25g/1oz of the butter in a frying pan, add the shallots and garlic and cook gently for about 10 minutes until softened. Pour the contents of the pan into the bowl of a food processor.

Return the pan to a high heat and add another 25g/1oz butter. Once really hot throw in the livers and sliced sage, season and cook for 1–2 minutes on each side, until browned on the outside but still pink in the middle. Tip the livers and their juices into the food processor, then pop the pan back on the heat.

Pour in the port and let it bubble and reduce by half then pour into the food processor with the livers and shallots. Blitz to a smooth purée then add 75g/2½oz of the butter, the cream, a grating of nutmeg and some seasoning. Blitz again until really smooth. Place a sieve over a serving bowl and use

ingredients and method continue overleaf...

★ ★ ★ ★ ★ ★ ★ ★ ★ ★ ★ ★ ★ ★ ★ ★ ★

★ ★

SHALLOT MARMALADE CHICKEN LIVER PÂTÉ

continued...

For the shallot marmalade
1 tbsp sunflower oil
100g/4oz shallots, finely sliced
75ml/2½fl oz port
1 heaped tbsp caster (granulated)
    sugar
2 tbsp red wine vinegar
pinch ground cinnamon

a spatula to push the warm pâté through. Pop the sage leaf on top. Melt the remaining butter, leave to cool a little, then pour over the top of the pâté, leaving any milky sediment behind. Chill for 1 hour.

For the shallot marmalade, heat the oil in a saucepan over a high heat. Add the shallots and cook for 3 minutes, then reduce the heat and cook for 15 minutes, stirring every so often, adding a little water if the shallots start to catch. Pour in the port and let it bubble and reduce until there is only a little left, then add the sugar, vinegar and cinnamon and season with salt. Cook gently for about 3 minutes until reduced and jam-like in consistency. Set aside to cool.

To make the toast, heat the grill to high. Place the bread on a baking tray and toast both sides. Cut off the crusts then slice in half horizontally so that you have two thin slices. Cut each slice into four triangles. Pop the triangles, untoasted side up, onto the baking tray and grill until golden brown. Top each slice with a spoonful of the pâté, a little shallot marmalade and a few micro leaves.

AVOCADO SALSA &
★
PORK PIBIL

Mexican food isn't all about heat. Pork pibil is a fragrant stewed-down braise that's almost like a rillette in texture. Make extra, you'll want the leftovers. In fact, make extra onions while you're at it – excellent with cheese.

MAKES 24 canapés

TAKES 3 hours, plus marinating

24 small slices cornbread
drizzle of olive oil
For the pork
1 dried ancho chilli, stalk removed and roughly chopped
1 tsp cumin seeds
1 tsp fennel seeds
4 cloves
8 black peppercorns
1 tbsp dried oregano
juice 2 oranges
juice 2 limes
2 tbsp cider vinegar
1 small red onion, roughly chopped
4 garlic cloves
700g/1lb 9oz pork shoulder steaks, cut into large chunks
salt and freshly ground black pepper

Heat a frying pan and add the ancho chilli, cumin and fennel seeds, cloves and peppercorns, then toast until smoky but not burnt. Transfer to a spice grinder or chopper and whizz to a powder. Add the oregano, citrus juices, vinegar, onion, garlic and season with salt and whizz until smooth.

Put the pork into a resealable food bag. Add the paste and massage into the meat. Pop in the fridge and leave to marinate for at least 2 hours, preferably overnight.

When ready to cook, preheat oven to 140°C fan/275°F/gas 3. Tip the contents of the food bag into a snug roasting tray. Pour over 100ml (3½fl oz) water and stir well. Cover tightly with foil and cook for 2–2½ hours, or until the meat is tender and shreds easily with two forks.

Meanwhile, make the pickled shallots. Tip the sugar, vinegar and some salt into a bowl, then stir until dissolved. Add the shallots, mix well and set aside for 30 minutes.

ingredients and method continue overleaf…

★ ★ ★ ★ ★ ★ ★ ★ ★ ★ ★ ★ ★ ★ ★ ★

★ ★

AVOCADO SALSA & PORK PIBIL
continued...

For the pickled shallots
  & salsa
2 tbsp caster (granulated) sugar
50ml/2fl oz red wine vinegar
2 shallots, very thinly sliced
½ large ripe avocado, peeled, stone
  removed, and finely chopped
good squeeze lime juice
handful coriander (cilantro)
  leaves, finely chopped

Once cooked, remove the meat from the roasting tray and shred the pork. Set aside. Tip the sauce into a saucepan and bring to the boil. Let it bubble for about 15 minutes until thickened and reduced. Mix the shredded meat into the sauce, taste, add some seasoning and set aside to cool a little.

As the sauce reduces, put the cornbread onto a baking tray, drizzle with oil and pop into the oven for 10–15 minutes or until toasted.

When ready to serve, quickly make the salsa by mixing the avocado, lime juice, coriander and some seasoning together in a bowl. Top each piece of toast with a spoonful of the shredded pork, a little salsa and a few rings of pickled shallot.

MINI CROQUE
★
MONSIEUR & MADAME

Gruyère guarantees a melting texture here while
the inauthentically Italian Parmesan adds
welcome cheesiness.

MAKES 12

TAKES 20 minutes

24 thin slices baguette
50g/2oz butter
25g/1oz plain (all-purpose) flour
185ml/6½fl oz milk
25g/1oz Parmesan, finely grated
75g/2½oz Gruyère, finely grated
freshly grated nutmeg
Dijon mustard, for spreading
6 slices good-quality wafer-thin
  smoked ham
drizzle of sunflower oil (optional)
6 quail's eggs (optional)
salt and freshly ground black
  pepper

Arrange the baguette slices on a baking tray. First make the béchamel. Melt the butter in a saucepan over a medium heat and brush one side of each slice with a little butter. Keep the pan on the heat and stir in the flour until a paste has formed. Gradually pour in the milk, whisking all the time, then bring to a simmer and let it bubble for 2 minutes. Stir through the Parmesan and 25g/1oz of the Gruyère until melted. Grate over a little nutmeg, then taste and season.

Heat the grill. Pop the bread slices under the grill and toast for 3 minutes or until golden brown. Take half the slices from the tray and set aside. Turn over the slices on the tray and spread with a little mustard. Tear the ham and divide between the slices, then top with the remaining Gruyère. Pop under the grill until the cheese has just melted. Place the reserved slices of baguette, untoasted side down, on top and push down gently. Spoon over the béchamel and return to the grill until bubbling. Leave to cool a little before serving.

To turn half of the toasted sandwiches into croques madames, heat a little oil in a frying pan. Crack in the quail's eggs and fry until the whites are set, then pop on top of the sandwiches.

TUNA

★

TARTARE

A steak 'tartare' is made with entirely raw meat that's carefully dressed. This tuna version is every bit as gorgeous but the lime and soy also partially 'cook' the fish in the style known as 'ceviche'.

🍴 MAKES 20–24 canapés

⏰ TAKES 25 minutes, plus freezing and chilling

200g/7oz sashimi grade tuna steak
2 tbsp sesame oil
20–24 thin slices baguette
1 avocado, halved and stone removed
1 red chilli, finely chopped
2 spring onions (scallions), finely chopped
2 tbsp light soy sauce
juice 1 lime
1 heaped tbsp black and white sesame seeds, toasted
24 small Thai basil leaves
salt and freshly ground black pepper

Place the tuna in the freezer for 30 minutes before you want to start making the tartare. Preheat the oven to 160°C fan/315°F/gas 4. Use 1 tbsp of the oil to brush each slice of bread, then place them on a baking tray. Bake for 6–8 minutes or until golden brown and crisp.

To make the tartare, remove the tuna from the freezer. Slice into matchstick strips then into ½cm/¼inch cubes and put into a bowl. Finely chop the avocado in the same way and add to the bowl. Throw in the chilli and spring onions, then stir through the soy sauce, lime juice and the remaining oil. Taste and season, then pop in the fridge and chill for 30 minutes.

Spoon the tartare onto the toast slices, sprinkle over the sesame seeds and top with Thai basil leaves.

SWEDISH
★
PRAWNS

There's a tradition of serving open sandwiches that spread across Scandinavia, and these elegant little canapés are topped with a Swedish-inspired combination of prawn and dill.

MAKES 18 crostini

TAKES 20 minutes

9 small slices pumpernickel bread, halved
2 tbsp olive oil
2 tbsp soured cream
3½ tbsp mayonnaise
½ red onion, finely chopped
good squeeze lemon juice
few dashes of Tabasco
small handful dill, finely chopped
250g/9oz cooked prawns (shrimp)
25g/1oz salmon caviar
salt and freshly ground black pepper

Preheat the oven to 160°C fan/315°F/gas 4. Brush both sides of each slice of bread with the oil, place on a baking tray and bake for 5–10 minutes, or until crisp. Remove and leave to cool.

Mix the soured cream, mayonnaise, onion, lemon juice, Tabasco and most of the dill in a bowl. Taste and season, then stir through the prawns.

Top the cooled toast slices with the prawn mixture and the remaining chopped dill, then finish with a spoonful of salmon caviar.

WHIPPED FETA WITH

★

BEETROOT & CARAWAY

Whipping up salty feta transforms it into a light, creamy spread that makes an ideal bed for the Russian-inspired combination of earthy beetroot and fragrant caraway.

🍴 MAKES 12 croutes

⏰ TAKES 35 minutes

2 medium beetroot, peeled
2 tbsp cider vinegar
1 tbsp rapeseed (canola) oil
1 tsp caster (granulated) sugar
zest 1 small orange and juice of ½
200g/7oz feta
2 tbsp Greek-style yoghurt
1 heaped tsp caraway seeds
12 small pieces granary bread
handful baby chard or sorrel
   leaves
salt and freshly ground black
   pepper

Cut the beetroot into matchsticks. Combine the vinegar, oil, sugar, orange zest and juice in a bowl with a good pinch of salt. Tip the beetroot into the bowl, stir well and set aside to pickle for at least 30 minutes, stirring every so often.

Meanwhile, crumble the feta into the small bowl of a food processor and whizz to a crumb. Spoon in the yoghurt and whizz for 3–4 minutes until smooth. Taste and season.

Toast the caraway seeds in a dry frying pan until aromatic. Toast the bread and, once cooled, top with the whipped feta. Drain the beetroot well then divide between the toast slices. Sprinkle over the caraway seeds and top with some baby chard or sorrel leaves.

PICKLED CUCUMBER &
★
HOT SMOKED SALMON

In Japanese home cooking these 'quick pickles', known as 'tsukemono', form a part of almost every meal. They take only minutes to prepare and once you've tried them, you'll never look at a raw vegetable the same way again.

🍴 MAKES 12

⏰ TAKES 35 minutes

¼ large cucumber, halved
    lengthways
5 radishes, very finely sliced
2 tsp caster (granulated) sugar
2½ tbsp white wine vinegar
140g/5oz full-fat cream cheese
2 tsp wholegrain mustard
6 slices rye bread, halved
    diagonally
2 fillets hot smoked salmon,
    skin removed
½ tbsp poppy seeds
12 edible flowers, such as violas
    (optional)
salt and freshly ground black
    pepper

Using a vegetable peeler or mandoline, slice the cucumber into ribbons and place in a bowl, then stir in the radishes, sugar, vinegar, a little salt and 3 tbsp water. Set aside to pickle for at least 30 minutes, stirring every so often.

Beat the cream cheese and mustard together in a bowl with some seasoning. Toast the bread slices and cool briefly, then spread with cream cheese. Drain the pickled vegetables and divide between the toast slices. Flake over the hot smoked salmon, sprinkle with poppy seeds and top with an edible flower, if using.

HORSERADISH
★
BEEF TARTARE

Partially freezing the beef makes it easier to cut thinly and does no harm to the texture or flavour. It's a really useful trick for making wafer-thin slices or, in this case, a fine hand-mince.

MAKES 24 canapés

TAKES 25 minutes, plus freezing

200g/7oz beef fillet steak
24 small squares challah bread
2 tbsp olive oil
1 tbsp capers, finely chopped
½ red onion, finely chopped
1 large gherkin, finely chopped
small handful parsley leaves,
    finely chopped
small handful chives, snipped
2 tsp mayonnaise
2 tsp tomato ketchup
few dashes of Tabasco
3–4 tbsp crème fraîche
small knob fresh horseradish,
    peeled
salt and freshly ground black
    pepper

Place the beef in the freezer for 30 minutes before you start making the tartare. Meanwhile, preheat the oven to 160°C fan/315°F/gas 4. Brush the pieces of bread with a little oil, place on a baking tray and bake for 6–8 minutes, or until crisp. Leave to cool.

Remove the beef from the freezer and slice into ½cm/¼inch strips, then finely dice each strip and place in a bowl. Add the capers, onion, gherkin, parsley and chives and stir well, then fold through the mayonnaise, ketchup, Tabasco and some seasoning. Chill until ready to serve.

Spoon the tartare onto the toast slices, top with a small dollop of crème fraîche and grate over some fresh horseradish.

CHICKEN LIVERS &
★
CRISP CHICKEN SKIN CROSTINI

There's something very pleasing about making something so elegant out of the bits of a chicken that most people throw away. Crisp chicken skin is dangerously addictive.

🍴 MAKES 12 crostini

⏰ TAKES 35 minutes

skin from 4 chicken breasts
12 slices ciabatta or sourdough
   bread
1 garlic clove, halved
100g/4oz pancetta cubes
1 shallot, finely diced
large knob butter
250g/9oz trimmed chicken livers,
   rinsed, patted dry and chopped
   into bite-sized pieces
2 tbsp Madeira
3 thyme sprigs, leaves picked,
   plus extra to serve
splash sherry vinegar
freshly ground black pepper

Preheat the oven to 180°C fan/350°F/gas 6. Place the chicken skin between two pieces of baking parchment. Pop on a baking tray and place a heavy roasting tray on top to press the skin down. Roast for about 15 minutes, or until very crisp. Set the skin aside to cool. Reserve the fat released from the chicken skin during cooking and use it to brush one side of the bread slices and place on a baking tray. Bake for 6–8 minutes until golden brown. Lightly rub each slice with the cut side of the garlic halves.

Tip the pancetta into a frying pan and set over a high heat. Cook for 1 minute, then add the shallot and cook for a further 3–4 minutes, until the pancetta is crisp and the shallot has softened.

Throw the butter into the pan with the shallots and once foaming add the chicken livers. Fry, stirring, for 3–4 minutes, until the livers are browned on the outside but pink in the middle. Splash in the Madeira and let it bubble until reduced by half. Stir through the thyme, vinegar and some black pepper, then pile onto the toast slices and drizzle over some of the cooking juices. Snap the chicken skin over the top, then scatter over a few thyme leaves.

SUPPER

★

TOASTS

PARMESAN PAIN PERDU

French toast is a favourite in diners and greasy spoons
all over the world but the truly posh call it 'pain perdu'.
Plenty of butter and long, slow stewing in wine make
the leeks meltingly spectacular.

SERVES 4

TAKES 30 minutes

50g/2oz butter
1 garlic clove, bashed
few thyme sprigs
75ml/2½fl oz white wine or water
3 leeks, trimmed, cut into 5cm/
    2 inch pieces then halved
    lengthways
3 large eggs
100ml/3½fl oz milk
25g/1oz Parmesan, finely grated,
    plus extra to serve
4 slices white farmhouse bread
salt and freshly ground black
    pepper

Place half the butter, the garlic, thyme and wine
or water in a shallow pan over a medium heat and
simmer until the butter has melted. Add the leeks,
gently toss in the buttery liquid and season with
salt and pepper. Cover and cook for 10 minutes.
Remove the lid and cook for a further 10 minutes
or until the leeks are tender and the liquid has
evaporated. Set aside to cool a little.

Meanwhile preheat the oven to 140°C fan/275°F/
gas 3.

In a jug, beat together the eggs, milk, grated
Parmesan and seasoning. Place the bread in a
shallow dish in a single layer and pour over the egg
mixture. Leave to soak for 5 minutes on each side.
Melt half of the remaining butter in a frying pan
over a low heat. Transfer two of the soaked bread
slices to the pan and fry for 2 minutes on each side,
or until golden brown. Transfer to a baking tray
and keep warm in the oven whilst you cook the
remaining slices in the same way.

Spoon the warm leeks over the eggy bread, top
with grated Parmesan and a little black pepper.

BLACK PUDDING

★

APPLE & HAZELNUT

The idea of sweet apple and nuts with black pudding might seem counterintuitive but the deep, earthy flavour of the pudding is a perfect foil. In Spanish cuisine black pudding is sometimes used with chocolate in desserts.

SERVES 4

TAKES 15 minutes

25g/1oz butter, plus extra for spreading
2 small cox apples
200g/7oz black pudding, roughly chopped
25g/1oz hazelnuts, very roughly chopped
5 sage leaves, finely sliced
drizzle of runny honey
4 slices poppy seed bloomer
salt and freshly ground black pepper

Melt the butter in a large frying pan. Quarter the apples, then remove the core and cut into ½cm/¼inch thick slices. Add to the pan and sprinkle over a little salt. Cook the apples gently, basting with the buttery juices for 2 minutes or until beginning to soften.

Push the apples to the side of the pan and turn up the heat. Throw in the black pudding and let it cook for about 3 minutes or until beginning to crisp and break up a little. Add the hazelnuts and sage to the pan and stir together. Continue to cook for a further minute or so, until the nuts have browned a little. Drizzle over the honey, season and toss everything together.

Toast the bread and butter well, then top with the black pudding and apple.

MUSHROOM

★

CHICKEN & TARRAGON

In a restaurant, this elegant fricassée of chicken and mushrooms would be served in a mound on a bone-china plate. But that's not the posh way. Heap it on toast and sprinkle with fresh tarragon. Much nicer, isn't it?

SERVES 4

TAKES 15 minutes

1 tbsp olive oil
2 large chicken breasts, cut into
   bite-sized chunks
250g/9oz wild mushrooms, such
   as chanterelle
85ml/3fl oz Marsala
125ml/4fl oz double (heavy) cream
large handful tarragon, finely
   chopped
4 slices spelt or wholemeal bread
salt and freshly ground black
   pepper

Heat the oil in a frying pan. Season the chicken then add to the pan and cook over a high heat for 3–4 minutes, until browned all over. Throw in the mushrooms and cook for 2–3 minutes or until they are beginning to wilt. Slosh in the Marsala and let it bubble for a few minutes until reduced by half. Stir in the cream and simmer for 2–3 minutes, until thickened slightly. Check for seasoning and finally stir through the tarragon, reserving a little for the garnish.

Toast the bread and top with the creamy mushrooms and chicken, then grind over a little black pepper and sprinkle over the reserved tarragon.

GREMOLATA &
★
BONE MARROW

Bone marrow is basically fat – delicious, rich, flavour-filled beef fat – and soaks into the toast in a way that will have you howling at the moon. Fortunately, gremolata is a sharp-flavoured and infinitely healthy combination of vegetable stuffs that entirely balances the marrow.

🍴 SERVES 4

⏰ TAKES 20 minutes

4 x 15cm/6 inch lengths bone marrow halves (about 700g/1lb 9oz total)
1 small red onion, very finely chopped
small bunch parsley, roughly chopped
2 tbsp capers, drained and roughly chopped
zest ½ lemon plus squeeze of juice
4–8 slices sourdough bread
salt and freshly ground black pepper

Preheat the oven to 180°C fan/350°F/gas 6. Place the bone marrow on a baking tray and roast in the hot oven for about 15–18 minutes, or until soft but not melting.

Meanwhile make the gremolata. In a bowl, combine the onion, parsley, capers, the lemon zest and juice and some seasoning. Toast the bread.

Remove the bone marrow from the oven and let everyone help themselves, scooping out the marrow and spreading it onto the toast then topping with spoonfuls of gremolata.

BUCK

★

RAREBIT

Most aficionados would argue that a good Welsh rarebit
cannot be improved upon. That's until you put an egg on
it. A fried egg can improve almost any food and in the
buck rarebit, it also creates a legendary hangover cure.

SERVES 6

TAKES 40 minutes

50g/2oz butter
50g/2oz plain (all-purpose) flour
250ml/9fl oz ale
175g/6oz mature (sharp) Cheddar,
  grated
3 tbsp crème fraîche
2 tsp English mustard
1 tbsp Worcestershire sauce
6 slices seeded bread
sunflower oil, for frying
6 eggs
handful pea shoots or baby leaf
  salad leaves
salt and freshly ground black
  pepper

Melt the butter in a saucepan and, once foaming,
add the flour and stir well to form a paste. Cook
for 30 seconds to 1 minute until bubbling. Gradually
whisk in the ale until you have a smooth thickish
sauce then let it bubble for 1–2 minutes. Add the
cheese, crème fraîche, mustard, Worcestershire
sauce and some seasoning and stir until melted and
combined. Set aside to cool and firm up a little.

Heat the grill to medium. Lightly toast the bread
then spread the cheese mixture thickly onto one
side. Pop under the grill for a few minutes, or until
golden and bubbling.

Meanwhile heat a little oil in a frying pan. Once hot
crack in three of the eggs and fry until the whites
are set but the yolks are still runny. Remove from
the pan and repeat with the remaining eggs. Pop
the fried eggs on top of the cheesy toast then
grind over some more black pepper to finish.
Serve with pea shoots or baby leaf salad leaves.

CHEESE

★

FONDUE

Anyone who's been skiing will recall the stomach-stretching excesses of the giant cheese fondue into which cubes of bread are dipped. The posh way to do this is to reverse the process. Smear the fondue on the toast and grill to bubbling perfection.

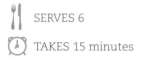

SERVES 6

TAKES 15 minutes

140g/5oz Comté, finely grated
140g/5oz Gruyère, finely grated
140g/5oz full-fat cream cheese
3–4 tbsp white wine
1 tbsp cornflour (cornstarch)
freshly grated nutmeg
6 slices granary bread
bunch radishes with their leaves
salt and freshly ground black
    pepper

Place the cheeses, wine, cornflour, a little nutmeg and some seasoning into the bowl of a food processor and whizz together. Taste and add more wine if needed.

Heat the grill and lightly toast the bread. Turn the grill down to its lowest setting. Spread the cheese mixture thickly over each slice of toast, then pop under the grill and let it gently melt and bubble for about 10 minutes. (Keep the grill on low as you want the cheese to melt slowly.) In the final minute of cooking, increase the heat to brown the top. Serve with crunchy radishes and their leaves.

DEVILLED
★
KIDNEYS

This dish originated in Edwardian gentlemen's clubs and was originally prepared in a silver chafing dish at the side of the dining table. It's worth the effort of preparing, partly because it's utterly gorgeous, partly because with its unique history, devilled kidneys are the very definition of 'Posh Toast'.

SERVES 2

TAKES 15 minutes

25g/1oz butter, plus extra for spreading
2 shallots, finely sliced
5 lamb's kidneys
2 slices sourdough bread
2 tbsp sweet sherry
3 tbsp double (heavy) cream
¼ tsp cayenne pepper
1 tsp Dijon mustard
dash Worcestershire sauce
small handful parsley, finely chopped
salt and freshly ground black pepper

Melt the butter in a frying pan over a medium heat. Add the shallots along with a pinch of salt and cook for about 5 minutes until softened. Meanwhile, prepare the kidneys. Halve them lengthways and snip out the white core, then wash under cold water and pat dry. Set aside.

Toast the bread and spread with butter. Add the kidneys to the pan with the shallots and let them cook and colour for about 2 minutes, until browned. (The kidneys should be browned on the outside and pink in the centre.) Splash in the sherry and let it bubble for a minute, then stir in the cream, cayenne, mustard, Worcestershire sauce and seasoning. Bring back to a simmer, then spoon over the hot buttered toast and scatter with parsley.

POSH

★

BEANS

There are some things you don't mess with. Tinned beans,
bright-orange and sloppy, are hard to beat, but these –
sticky, sweet and spicy – just might make you
change your mind.

SERVES 6

TAKES 1 hour

2 tbsp sunflower oil
8 rashers smoked streaky bacon,
  snipped into pieces
1 onion, finely chopped
3 garlic cloves, peeled and bashed
25g/1oz dark muscovado sugar
2 tbsp treacle (molasses)
100ml/3½fl oz cider vinegar
2 tsp mustard powder
500g/1lb 2oz tomato passata
1 shot espresso
400g/14oz tin haricot (navy) beans,
  rinsed and drained
400g/14oz tin pinto beans, rinsed
  and drained
6 slices white farmhouse bread
butter, for spreading
salt and freshly ground black
  pepper

Heat the oil in a large heavy-based pan or casserole
dish over a high heat. Add the bacon to the pan
and cook for about 8 minutes until just starting
to crisp. Tip in the onion and cook gently for 5
minutes, until softened. Add the garlic and cook for
30 seconds, followed by the sugar and treacle, and
stir until dissolved.

Stir in the vinegar, mustard powder, passata and
espresso. Bring the boil and simmer for 20 minutes,
or until thickened. Tip in the drained beans and
cook gently for 15–20 minutes to let the flavours
develop. Add a little water if the sauce becomes
too thick, taste and season.

Toast the bread and spread with butter, then spoon
over the beans.

NOT TINNED
★
SARDINES

Sardines on toast used to be a storecupboard favourite but these days fresh sardines are easy to find. This elegant version is redolent of a Mediterranean mini-break, but if you're feeling nostalgic you can crack open a tin.

SERVES 4

TAKES 25 minutes

2 tbsp extra virgin olive oil
2 shallots, finely sliced
1 tsp caster (granulated) sugar
1 small garlic clove, crushed
325g/11oz cherry tomatoes
1 tbsp tomato purée (paste)
1 tbsp sherry vinegar
6 butterflied sardines, small bones removed
4 slices brown bread
salt and freshly ground black pepper

Heat 1 tbsp of the oil in a frying pan, add the shallots and cook gently for 5 minutes or until softened. Sprinkle over the sugar, add the garlic and cook for 30 seconds, until the sugar has melted. Tip the tomatoes into the pan and cook for about 8 minutes, until softened. Add a splash of water if the shallots are on the edge of burning.

Squash the tomatoes down with the back of a wooden spoon or a fork, then stir in the tomato purée and 3 tbsp water. Cook gently for a further 5 minutes, then add the vinegar and some seasoning. Set aside whilst you cook the sardines.

Heat ½ tbsp of the oil in a large frying pan. Halve each butterflied sardine so that you have 12 fillets. Place 6 fillets in the hot pan, skin-side down and cook for 1–2 minutes, until golden and crispy, then carefully turn over and cook for 30 seconds. Remove from the pan and repeat with the remaining fillets.

Toast the bread and spoon over the tomato sauce. Top with the sardines, drizzle over the remaining oil and grind over a little black pepper.

SCOTCH

★

WOODCOCK

Scotch woodcock isn't remotely Scottish and doesn't contain any woodcock but it's a British classic. Make far too much of the anchovy-flavoured butter. It makes a marvellous breakfast when spread thickly on toast.

SERVES 2

TAKES 15 minutes

8 anchovy fillets in extra virgin olive oil, drained
25g/1oz butter, softened, plus a little extra for frying
few pinches cayenne pepper, plus a little extra to serve
few pinches ground cinnamon
few pinches ground ginger
freshly grated nutmeg
4 eggs
2 tbsp double (heavy) cream
2 slices spelt bread
small handful chives, snipped
salt and freshly ground black pepper

Finely chop four of the anchovies, then mash in a bowl together with the softened butter, the spices and a little black pepper. Set aside.

Melt a small knob of butter in a saucepan over a very low heat. Crack the eggs into a bowl and whisk lightly with a fork. Season with black pepper and a very small pinch of salt. Tip the eggs into the pan and stir gently every so often, until just beginning to set. Remove from the heat and stir through the cream. Return to the heat and cook for a further 30 seconds to 1 minute until almost set but still soft. Remove from the heat.

Meanwhile, toast the bread and spread with the anchovy spiced butter. Top with the scrambled eggs, remaining anchovies, snipped chives and a final pinch of cayenne pepper.

TURKEY
★
STROGANOFF

In the Middle Ages food was served on 'trenchers', plate-sized slices of bread that could be eaten after use. Toast creates a support structure so you can eat something gorgeous, messily and with your hands. Turkey stroganoff is a good starting point, but once you get going, you'll be serving all kinds of things on a big toast 'trencher'.

🍴 SERVES 4

⏰ TAKES 25 minutes

2 tbsp sunflower oil, plus an extra
    drizzle
2 tbsp plain (all-purpose) flour
400g/14oz turkey breast strips
1 large onion, finely sliced
2 garlic cloves, crushed
1 tbsp smoked paprika, plus extra
    to sprinkle
1 tbsp tomato purée (paste)
275ml/9½fl oz chicken stock
1 heaped tsp wholegrain mustard
150ml/5fl oz soured cream
4 slices sourdough bread
handful parsley, roughly chopped
salt and freshly ground black
    pepper

Heat 1 tbsp of the oil in a shallow pan. Tip the flour into a bowl and season well. Toss the turkey strips in the flour. Fry the turkey in the hot oil in two batches for 5 minutes, until browned and crispy in places, adding the remaining oil, if needed. Remove using a slotted spoon and set aside.

Return the pan to the heat, add a drizzle of oil and throw in the onion. Cook gently for about 8 minutes until softened, then stir in the garlic. Sprinkle over the paprika and squeeze in the tomato purée. Stir, then pour over the hot stock. Bring to a simmer and return the turkey and any juices to the pan. Cook for 5 minutes, until the sauce has thickened and the meat is cooked. Stir in the mustard and about a third of the soured cream, season and gently warm through.

Toast the bread, then spoon over the stroganoff. Dollop the remaining soured cream on top, then scatter over the parsley and, if you like, a little more paprika.

HAGGIS & WHISKY ONIONS

We usually only see haggis at big ceremonial Burns Night suppers, but its intense flavours work really well in more elegant executions. Only a small amount is needed to combine with the rich egg yolk in a posh topping.

SERVES 4

TAKES 45 minutes

2½ tbsp olive oil
3 large onions, thinly sliced
½ heaped tsp dark brown sugar
50ml/2fl oz whisky
400g/14oz haggis
4 slices sourdough bread
4 duck eggs
salt and freshly ground black
   pepper

Heat 2 tbsp of the oil in a frying pan, add the onions and a few pinches of salt and cook gently for 30 minutes, stirring every so often, until softened and starting to brown. Turn up the heat and cook for a further 5 minutes. Sprinkle over the sugar and pour in the whisky. Stir for a few more minutes until the onions are nicely browned but not burnt.

Meanwhile cook the haggis according to the packet instructions. Tip into a frying pan and brown over a medium-high heat until crispy in places, adding a little oil if needed. Toast the bread and top with the sticky onions and haggis. Heat the remaining glug of oil in the frying pan, then crack in two of the eggs and fry until the whites have set but the yolks are still runny. Repeat with the remaining eggs, then place on top of the haggis toast.

CHINESE PRAWN TOAST

Prawn toast has always been the easy starter with a takeaway meal, but that doesn't do the dish justice. Made from scratch and poshed up with pickled cucumber and chilli jam, it's a meal in itself.

SERVES 6

TAKES 45 minutes

140g/5oz shelled and deveined raw king prawns (jumbo shrimp)
1 tsp grated ginger
2 spring onions (scallions), sliced
1 tsp light soy sauce
1 egg white
2 tsp cornflour (cornstarch)
½ cucumber
2½ tbsp rice vinegar
2 tsp caster (granulated) sugar
sunflower oil, for frying
5 slices white farmhouse bread, crusts removed
3 tbsp sesame seeds
6 tbsp chilli jam
salt and freshly ground black pepper

Place the prawns, ginger, spring onions, soy sauce, egg white, cornflour and some seasoning into the small bowl of a food processor. Blitz to a smooth paste and chill for 30 minutes.

Meanwhile use a vegetable peeler or mandoline to slice the cucumber into ribbons. Measure the vinegar and sugar into a bowl and add a little salt. Stir to dissolve, then toss through the cucumber. Set aside to pickle.

Fill a shallow frying pan 1cm/½inch deep with oil then set over a medium heat. Spread each slice of bread thickly with the prawn mixture. Sprinkle over the sesame seeds and lightly press down. Cut each slice of bread into three or four long strips.

Test a small piece of bread in the hot oil – it should brown in about 40 seconds. If you have a thermometer, the oil should have reached 180°C/350°F. Once the oil is hot enough fry the slices in batches, for 1–2 minutes on each side, until golden brown. Drain on kitchen paper. Serve with the pickled cucumber and chilli jam.

LABNEH

★

MANEESH FLATBREAD

You'll make more labneh than you need for the flatbreads. Keep it covered in the fridge for up to a week and use it to top salads, as a dip, or serve with spiced roast lamb.

🍴 SERVES 2

⏰ TAKES 20 minutes, plus 8 hours straining

500g/1lb 2oz 10% fat Greek-style yoghurt
½ garlic clove, crushed
2 tbsp extra virgin olive oil, plus extra to drizzle
2½ tbsp za'atar
2 flatbreads
25g/1oz pistachios
2 handfuls mint leaves
½ tsp sumac
salt and freshly ground black pepper

First make the labneh. Mix the yoghurt and ½ tsp salt together in a bowl. Line a sieve with muslin cloth or cheesecloth and spoon in the yoghurt. Gather up the ends of the cloth and suspend the sieve over a bowl. Place in the fridge and leave to strain for about 8 hours, until thickened.

Preheat the oven to 180°C fan/350°F/gas 6. Spoon 200g/7oz of the labneh into a bowl and stir through the crushed garlic. In a separate bowl, mix together the oil, za'atar and some seasoning. Place the flatbreads on a baking tray and spread with the za'atar mixture. Dollop over spoonfuls of the garlic labneh and spread it out a little. Cook in the oven for 10–12 minutes, until the breads are golden and crisp. Tip the pistachios onto a small baking tray and toast in the oven for 8 minutes with the flatbreads. Leave to cool, then roughly chop.

Allow the flatbreads to cool for a moment, then scatter over the pistachios, mint leaves, sumac and a little drizzle of oil.

SPICED
★
POTTED CRAB

Fans of the flashy lobster often forget how delicious fresh crab can be. The white meat is particularly sweet and fresh-tasting and when poshed-up with some subtle curry flavourings, it's just shockingly good.

 SERVES 4

TAKES 40 minutes

200g/7oz fresh white crabmeat
100g/4oz butter
½ red chilli, deseeded and finely chopped
2 spring onions (scallions), white and green parts, very finely sliced
small handful coriander (cilantro) leaves, finely chopped, plus extra to serve
zest and juice ½ lime (keep the other half to serve)
few pinches curry powder
3 tbsp Greek-style yoghurt
4–8 thin slices brown bread
salt and freshly ground black pepper

Pick through the crab to make sure it contains no shell, then place in a bowl. Melt half the butter in a small pan and leave to cool. Stir the chilli, spring onions, finely chopped coriander, the lime zest and juice, curry powder, yoghurt and some seasoning into the crabmeat. Stir in the cooled butter. Pack into a jar or bowl. Melt the remaining butter, then leave to cool a little before spooning off any scum from the surface. Pour over the crab, leaving any milky solids behind in the pan. Leave to set in the fridge for about 30 minutes.

When ready to eat, toast the bread and spread with the potted crab. Scatter over some coriander leaves and serve with lime wedges to squeeze over.

HORSERADISH CREAM &

★

GRILLED OX HEART

Ox heart sounds offally but it's actually a clean, fat-free and well-worked muscle. It has an excellent steaky flavour and should be flash-fried rare. This allows juices to flow that are conveniently caught by the toast beneath.

🍴 SERVES 2

⏰ TAKES 10 minutes

250g/9oz ox heart
1 tbsp creamed horseradish
3 tbsp crème fraîche
2 slices sourdough bread
1 tbsp olive oil
handful watercress leaves
6 cornichons, halved lengthways
salt and freshly ground black
   pepper

Remove any fat or sinew from the ox heart and thinly slice. Set aside. In a bowl, combine the horseradish, crème fraîche and some seasoning.

Heat a griddle pan over high heat. Drizzle the bread with 1 tsp of the oil and toast both sides on the hot griddle. Season the ox heart, rub with the remaining oil and griddle for 30 seconds to 1 minute on each side, depending on how thick your slices are — it should be charred on the outside and pink in the middle. Transfer to a plate and leave to rest for a few minutes.

Divide the griddled ox heart and watercress leaves between the slices of toast. Spoon over the horseradish cream and top with the cornichons and a little black pepper.

CAULIFLOWER
★
CHEESE

Cauliflower cheese is an old-school comfort food favourite and is an ideal candidate for the posh treatment. With the florets poached to softness and a rich and creamy Mornay sauce, they become the perfect addition to a crisp slice of toasted seed bread.

SERVES 4

TAKES 18 minutes

1 small cauliflower (about 600g/1lb 5oz), broken into small florets
25g/1oz butter, plus extra for spreading
25g/1oz plain (all-purpose) flour
300ml/11fl oz milk
200g/7oz grated mature (sharp) Cheddar
1 tsp English mustard
1 egg yolk
4 slices caraway or seeded bread
freshly grated nutmeg
few handfuls watercress (optional)
salt and freshly ground black pepper

Bring a large pan of water to the boil. Drop in the cauliflower florets and simmer for 5 minutes, or until tender. Drain and set aside.

Melt the butter in small saucepan over a medium heat. Stir in the flour to form a paste. Gradually pour in the milk, whisking all the time until you have a smooth sauce. Bring to a simmer, keep whisking, and let it bubble for 2 minutes, until thickened. Add most of the Cheddar, the mustard and some seasoning. Stir until melted, then remove from the heat and pop in the egg yolk. Stir to combine, then fold through the cauliflower.

Heat the grill to medium. Lay the bread on a baking tray, and lightly toast both sides. Spread with butter then divide the cauliflower between the slices. Sprinkle over the remaining cheese and pop under the grill for a few minutes, until golden and bubbling. Finish with a good grating of fresh nutmeg. Serve with watercress leaves, if liked.

Supper Toasts

WARM HUMMUS &
★
SPICED LAMB

In Lebanon, flatbread topped with hummus and spiced ground lamb is called lahmacun and is served as a popular street food. Use good-quality shop-bought hummus if you're feeling lazy.

SERVES 4

TAKES 20 minutes

400g/14oz tin chickpeas, drained and rinsed
3 tbsp tahini
2 garlic cloves, crushed
zest ½ lemon and juice 1 small lemon
1 tsp ground cumin
2 tbsp natural yoghurt
3 tbsp olive oil
2 tbsp pine nuts
large knob butter
400g/14oz minced (ground) lamb
1½ tsp ground allspice
1 tsp ground cinnamon
4 slices wholemeal bread
½ tsp chilli (hot pepper) flakes (use Aleppo or Turkish chilli flakes if you can find them)
large handful parsley leaves, roughly chopped
salt and freshly ground black pepper

Preheat the oven to 160°C fan/315°F/gas 4.

Place the chickpeas, tahini, 1 garlic clove, the lemon zest and juice, cumin, yoghurt, 2 tbsp oil and 2 tbsp cold water into a food processor. Season, then blend for about 5 minutes until completely smooth. Transfer to an ovenproof dish. Heat a frying pan and add the pine nuts, tossing until they start to colour. Add the butter and let it melt and turn golden. Pour the buttery mixture over the hummus and bake in the oven for 10 minutes.

Meanwhile, heat the remaining oil in the same frying pan over a high heat. Add the lamb and cook for about 8 minutes, stirring, until the lamb is browned and crisp and any liquid evaporated. Stir through the remaining garlic, allspice, cinnamon, season, and cook for 2 minutes.

Toast the bread. Spoon the warm hummus over the toast. Scoop up the spiced lamb with a slotted spoon and divide between the slices of toast. Top with a sprinkling of chilli flakes and some parsley.

SAUSAGES &
★
LENTILS

Puy lentils have a good strong flavour all of their own and are often cooked slowly with sausages to make a warm and sustaining one-pot dish. Toast made from an Italian or French rustic country bread is the ideal receiver for their flavour-filled juices.

SERVES 4

TAKES 1 hour

2 tbsp extra virgin olive oil, plus extra to drizzle
8 chipolatas or small pork sausages
1 onion, finely chopped
2 garlic cloves, crushed
1 small carrot, finely chopped
2 celery sticks, finely chopped
1 tsp fennel seeds
125g/4½oz Puy lentils
3 rosemary sprigs, leaves picked
450ml/16fl oz hot chicken or vegetable stock
2 tsp Dijon mustard
4 slices sourdough or rustic country bread
salt and freshly ground black pepper

Heat the oil in a large frying pan over a medium heat and briefly brown the sausages on all sides. Remove the sausages and set aside on a plate, keeping the pan on the heat. Turn the heat down, tip the onion into the pan and soften gently for 5 minutes. Add the garlic, carrot and celery and cook for 10 minutes until softened. Add the fennel seeds and stir for 1 minute, then tip in the lentils and rosemary and stir well. Pour over the hot stock then cover and simmer gently for 20 minutes.

Nestle the sausages amongst the lentils and cook, covered, for a further 10 minutes. Remove the lid, turn up the heat and cook for a final 5 minutes. Once the liquid has been absorbed, the lentils are tender and the sausages cooked, stir through the mustard and some seasoning.

Toast the bread. For each slice of toast, spoon over the lentils and two sausages then drizzle with a little extra oil.

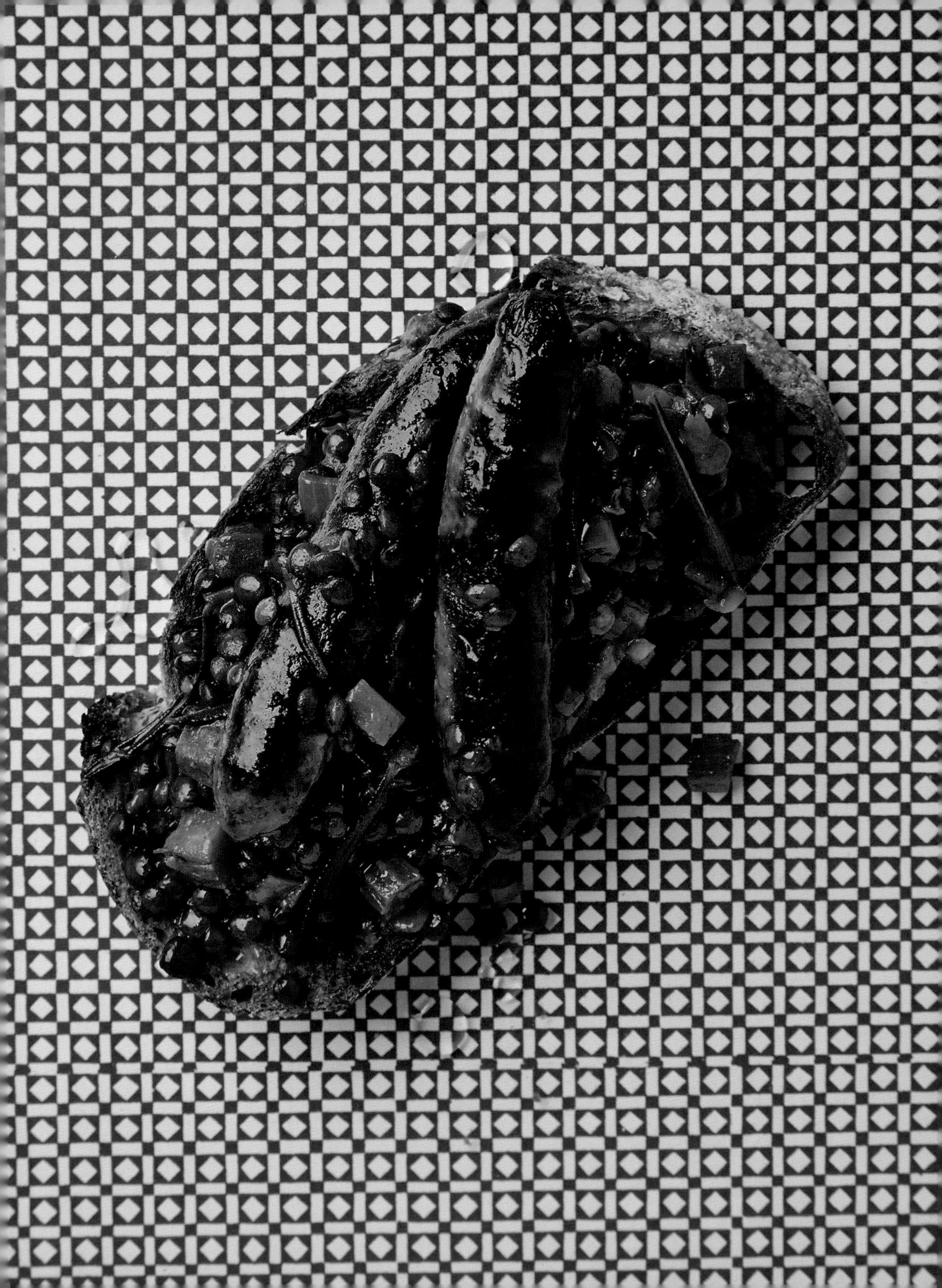

INDEX

★★★

THANK YOU

Posh Toast was a real team effort.
To Tim Hayward for all the words, ideas
and advice. To Emily Kydd for turning
a mad list of dishes into fantastic
recipes. To Louise Hagger for her
brilliant photography and styling.
To Kate Wanwimolruk for the snappy
edit. And to everyone at Quadrille for
making it happen: especially Helen,
Gemma, Harriet, Inez, Margaux,
Vincent and Tom.

Sarah